LIFE, DEATH, AND
THE BITS IN BETWEEN

Michael Collins

Life, Death, and
the Bits in Between

the columba press

First published in 2014 by
the columba press
55A Spruce Avenue, Stillorgan Industrial Park,
Blackrock, Co. Dublin

Cover by David Mc Namara
Origination by The Columba Press
Illustrations by Joe Connolly
Printed in Ireland by SPRINT-Print Ltd

ISBN 978 1 78218 133 0

Contents

A Time of Innocence

A Bishop Calls

The Parish Priest's temper had reached ignition point over the visit of the new Bishop, and his curates were showing a predictable lack of interest in the entire affair.

Their obvious ignorance of the scriptural warning to kings who go up against the enemy, to pick someone smaller than themselves, had not registered, for in similar vein a priest – and especially a curate – who went up against his bishop either by thought, word or deed and especially by omission, could expect to get it in the neck; and sadly, when curates got it in the neck, parish priests tended to feel the pain.

The red piping on his clerical soutane, the emblem of his high position as a Canon of the Diocese, quivered at the thought, and he made one more despairing attempt to breach the walls of their indifference.

'You must surely have some idea what he likes to eat. Weren't you in the seminary with him for five years?'

The Senior Curate laid aside his newspaper with an elaborate show of patience, and addressed his superior, much as a severely tried father might address his persistent but feeble-minded son.

'As I have explained already, Father, in exhaustive detail, he displayed no particular preference for any item of diet during his days in college, due no doubt to the fact that, like the rest of us, he had nothing to express any preference about, and had to make do with what was laid before him – or decline and diminish from starvation. I see no reason to assume that he has departed from this fundamental, and I may say admirable, principle of eating what is set before him, and I can think of no sufficiently cogent reason why we should attempt to persuade him to do so at this juncture.'

The Senior Curate had read a lot of books in his time, and tended to address everyone like a public meeting.

'Well, that's not much help,' snapped the Parish Priest.

The Junior Curate was a nervous young man, with a scrupulous turn of mind, and he questioned the morality of leaving his parish priest in such acute, though uncalled for, distress, without doing something to alleviate it.

'Perhaps we could start the dinner with smoked salmon,' he ventured. 'It was served at Bishop Tracey's Ordination dinner.'

'Smoked salmon,' said the Parish Priest blankly. 'What kind of stuff is that?'

'It is thin slices of salmon that has been smoked over an oakwood fire.'

'I dunno,' said the Parish Priest vaguely. 'Mary Ann is not a great hand at cooking these fancy dishes.'

'Oh, you don't cook it,' said the Junior Curate. 'You eat it raw.'

'What?' barked the Parish Priest, and his voice started to climb the scale into what the Senior Curate had once described as his 'hysterical mode'.

'What? Are you mad? The Bishop is coming to the parish for the first time in his life, and you want me to feed him raw fish.'

The Junior Curate abruptly closed his mouth, and reproved himself severely for ever having opened it. Fraternal charity might indeed be like oil running down the collar of one's robe, but his boss had just cut off the supply.

His senior colleague merely returned to his newspaper with an air of languid superiority and a prolonged and meaningful sigh. The Parish Priest flicked his gaze from one to the other, finally aware that he had just buried all hope of further discussion, and then turned on his heel and left.

The conversation at the episcopal table was dying a slow and painful death. The Bishop dragged it bodily up one avenue after another in the plaintive hope that someone would follow him, but the Senior Curate was doing his bored intellectual bit, the Junior Curate had taken a vow of silence as an alternative to saying the wrong thing, and the Parish Priest was watching the Bishop so closely for signs of dissatisfaction with the dinner that he heard nothing of what was being said.

The Bishop finally decided to adopt the direct approach, and aimed his questions first at the Junior Curate.

'And how many years are you ordained, Father?'

'Two, M'Lord,' replied the Junior Curate. 'Three next June.'

The Bishop gazed at him with all the innocence of a cobra in a hen house. 'And has your experience of the clerical life lived up to your expectations?' he asked.

The Junior Curate started like one of the aforesaid hens and tried to avoid the fangs. 'Well, some things are a bit different. I mean, some of the clergy, for example, are a bit different from what I expected.'

'Ah, I see. You feel that they would give a better account of themselves if they conformed more to your own ideal of the priesthood?'

The Junior Curate fluttered around in panic, looking for an escape hatch. 'Oh, no. No M'Lord, I didn't mean it that way. O ... !'

The Bishop dropped him smoothly from the conversation by turning to the Senior Curate. 'And has your significantly greater experience, Father, led you to a different conclusion?'

The Senior Curate was no chicken. Indeed, he was more of a clerical mongoose, and bishops did not frighten him. 'In common with the poet Donne, Bishop, I find comparisons odious. If the generality of the clergy have difficulty framing even a coherently grammatical sentence it does not follow that those who can are intellectual or artistic giants. I prefer to abide by my own standards of excellence and leave those who must to struggle with their grammar as best they can. No doubt they are content with popular acclaim in other fields of endeavour such as sport or, what is loosely termed nowadays, entertainment.'

The Bishop did not bat an eyelid but smoothly picked up the gauntlet. 'May I ask what standards then you would apply to your own humble efforts say in the art of letter writing?'

'If a model must be named then I think I would tend to emulate the gifts of the Marchioness de Sévigné in her letters to her daughter,' said the Senior Curate, and though his acquaintance with Madame de Sévigné was distinctly superficial he could not help adding under his breath, 'Let's see you catch that one with your crozier!'

But catch it his Lordship did; and he also returned it with some force. 'One would hesitate to classify the exchange of idle gossip between Madame de Sévigné and the Countess de Grignan as noteworthy literature.'

This stymied the Senior Curate for a moment, but when it came to chancing his arm he had a head start on both fools and angels. 'Whatever judgement may be passed on her letters to the Countess de Grignan, I find her letters to her daughter to be both subtle and polished.'

'Strange,' murmured the Bishop, quietly yet distinctly. 'I was under the impression that the Countess de Grignan in fact was her daughter.'

The Parish Priest had listened goggle-eyed to this exchange. He could hardly believe his ears. For the first time in living memory his Senior Curate had been flattened. That was the only word for it. Flattened! How he would enjoy telling this one at the next clerical conference.

The reverie was broken only by the sudden realisation that the Bishop was talking to him.

'Oh, very sorry, M'Lord, what was that you were saying?' They had got to the coffee and biscuits stage by this time and he had high hopes that he had got the menu right after all, for the Bishop had duly eaten everything that was laid down before him. 'I said, would you ever have a spot of jam about the house?'

Jam, thought the Parish Priest. He wants jam. You tramp the feet off yourself around supermarkets buying every kind, shape and smell of cheese that ever was invented, and he wants jam on his biscuits! No doubt about it! He was out to get all three of them. Different weapons maybe, but the same tactics.

'Jam?' he said. 'Jam. Certainly, M'Lord. A spot of jam.'

He bolted from the table and disappeared in the direction of the kitchen, calling loudly for Mary Ann to bring jam, but his voice gradually faded into silence, for search as he might every cupboard in the kitchen, to the monotonous accompaniment of Mary Ann's lamentation, 'I did buy jam Father, I did buy jam,' not a trace of jam could be found on the premises.

However, the Parish Priest had been to the edge of the world before now. He had faced the abyss and survived, so he knew well the importance of being prepared – for everything. Plan B was called into action.

At the front of the house sat Joe McPeake, the local taxi man, in his gleaming black Cortina, engine turning over every fifteen minutes, as per the Canon's instructions, like a Tiger Tank in the Russian snows, ready to take off at a moment's notice. The message was relayed to him by a now tearful Mary Ann. Fly like the wind to the village and fetch jam. What kind of jam? Any kind of jam. Any quantity of jam. Jam in any kind of receptacle or container. Just hasten like winged Mercury, the messenger of the gods, and stop for neither man, beast nor guardian of the law, until he had produced jam of some sort. The Bishop wanted jam.

Joe was geared more to ostentation than to performance, his speciality being the delivery of brides to the church twenty minutes late; but he did his best.

His best was not good enough, however.

By the time he had made his purchase – one pound of Robertson's Mixed Fruit Jam on special offer at 39p – and returned to base, the presbytery was deserted. Bishop, Parish Priest, curates and Housekeeper had all disappeared, gone no doubt to the Church for confirmations, and the broken remnants of the dinner still lay on the table.

Joe stood for a moment, like the late Ozymandias, king of kings, surveying the rubble, weighing up the situation and, jam in hand, considering possible courses of action. After some concentrated mental effort he pulled a chair up to the table, poured himself a cup of coffee, laced the remaining biscuits with a generous coating of Robertson's Mixed Fruit Jam, and fell to.

The confirmation ceremony was well under way, and going smoothly. The Parish Priest was confined by liturgical necessity to his seat in the Sanctuary, but he kept an eagle eye on everything that transpired below, especially now that the Bishop had departed from the script and was inviting doctrinal opinions from the floor. The Parish Priest had heard of this dangerous practice and had warned his teachers to impose silence, if needs be by threats of physical violence on all but the most intelligent candidates. Nonetheless, he rose in the air like an anxious hen every time a voice was raised from the pews in response to the Bishop's questions. The gifts of the Holy Spirit and the effects of the sacrament of Conformation were duly explored without mishap, and the Parish Priest relaxed into his chair with an audible sigh of relief as the Bishop finally turned to the altar and began the prayers.

They had made it. It was plain sailing from here on in.

His sense of relief was so overpowering that the problem with the thurible might have escaped his attention but for the intervention of the Bishop's secretary in the role of Master of Ceremonies. The movement caught his subconscious eye and he stiffened like a pointer. The Bishop, the Altar Boy and the Secretary were all wrestling with the lid of the thurible, the metal pot containing hot charcoal and incense, which for some unknown reason appeared to have chosen this one occasion in its entire career to lock itself solidly to the base. They were making heavy weather of a simple problem, it seemed to the Parish Priest because they were handling the thurible very gingerly and merely tickling the lid with the tips of their fingers – or so it appeared. He suffered their incompetence in silence for as long as he could, and then darted between the Altar Boy and the Bishop and grasped the thurible solidly in both hands.

'F***!' screamed the Parish Priest, sending incense and red-hot charcoal flying in all directions.

It was not the word itself, for it was fully familiar to all the congregation, nor was it the volume at which it was unleashed, for they had experienced the Parish Priest's vocal powers in full flight on many an occasion, but a combination of circumstances – the solemnity of the occasion, the company in which it was uttered, and the indiscretion of the Parish Priest in touching a thurible which had sat through a Bishop's sermon and was now red-hot – somehow they all now combined to turn an unfortunate mishap into a liturgical landmark.

The silence could be heard in the next townland. The Bishop bowed his head in silent prayer, and kept it bowed. The Altar Boys grinned knowingly at one another. The Parish Priest busied himself furiously with the scattered contents of the thurible and hid his blushes as best he could. It was left to his clerical confrères in the front row to break the silence, which they did with a ragged explosion of strangled groans, like a flock of demented sheep. It took much shushing from the senior clergy plus menacing looks and even the threat of ecclesiastical sanctions before order was restored. The Bishop took an inordinately long time over his silent prayer and in the meantime the Parish Priest sat and sucked his wounded fingers.

When Mass was ended and they had all returned to the sacristy, there was a strained and uncomfortable silence. Eventually the Bishop thanked him for his hospitality and departed with no reference by word or gesture to what had happened. The accompanying clergy followed his example and under cover of the Bishop's departure put as much distance as possible between themselves and the battlefield.

The Parish Priest was last to leave. He set his feet towards the presbytery, severely alone, teeth clenched, and ready to kill. He was met in the dining room by Joe McPeake holding in his hand a generously jam-laden biscuit.

'I got ye yer jam, Father.'

To this day Joe loyally maintains that he must have been mistaken. The Parish Priest would never use language like that!

The two curates trundled in a little later, like a pair of disillusioned Jacobites after the Battle of the Boyne. Their own downfall at the hands of the Bishop had added some spice to their boss's adventure, but they quickly learned that while victory is personal, defeat is social. They found themselves lumped alongside the Parish Priest by their clerical confrères as corporate conveyors of mirth to the diocese, and they were still smarting from it. They were also confused by the strange discovery that they bore a certain loyalty to their parish priest and took a dim view of outsiders who usurped their unique right to laugh at him. The whole day, in fact had been most confusing. They had suffered at the hands of all manner of clergy, their supposed brothers in the ministry, and yet it was hard to see what they could have done to avoid it.

The Parish Priest, however, could see clearly what could have been done.

He faced them in the hallway and rasped, 'Well?'

They looked blankly at him.

'Well? Maybe now you'll pay attention to what a bishop likes to eat. None of this would have happened if we had known what kind of thing he likes.'

They looked at one another like lost souls, finally despairing of salvation.

Anything was possible. For all they knew, he could be right.

'Well, that's not much help,' snapped the Parish Priest.

Clerical Conscripts

'Right boys,' said the Parish Priest. 'The readings.'

The 'boys' regarded him glumly. Three of them were over sixty, one of them was the same age as the Parish Priest himself, and the other was a rapidly ageing forty-three. 'Joe,' he said, 'you take the first one. It's a nice wee short one.'

Joe did not display any obvious signs of joy over the brevity of the reading, especially when he noticed that it was from the Song of Songs. He took a dim view of any form of sexual exhibitionism, especially in the Bible. Apart from anything else, he felt distinctly uncomfortable in his cream-coloured concelebration alb. The zipper at his left ear had stuck halfway and the ends of it poked up in different directions like a pair of rudely raised fingers.

He looked the reading over briefly and muttered, 'Hmphm!'

'Billy, will you take the responsorial psalm. We'll stick to "The Lord is my Shepherd". That "Listen O Daughter, give ear to my words' only confuses people".'

Billy was in full agreement. He was only five-feet-two, and in a strange alb he looked like Dopey out of the Seven Dwarfs. He figured he had enough natural handicaps to contend with, never mind exotic responsorial psalms.

'Jamie, would you take the second reading. First Corinthians. About celibacy. Though damn the bit need there was for St Paul to tell men who have wives to live as though they had none. Half the parish is doing it already.'

Jamie was unmoved by this flash of clerical wit. He felt ill at ease in his 'maternity smock' as he called it. He was used to an old-fashioned alb with a tightly knotted cincture that pulled himself and the garment into shape.

'In these outfits I keep thinking I've forgotten to put me trousers on,' he complained.

There were three other concelebrants in the background wearing a series of outfits that reflected the history rather than the present state of the liturgical movement. All had amices wrapped around their necks, with varying degrees of success, and one had the stole crossed over his chest so that he looked like a well-armed Mexican bandit.

The Parish Priest accepted it all with equanimity, but he drew the line when one of them produced a biretta and perched it on his bald head 'to keep the heat in'. He was tempted to urge the wearer in fairly blunt language to catch himself on, but he made do with a diplomatic suggestion that it might 'unbalance' the procession if only one man turned up wearing headgear.

Having completed the inspection, he helloed to the altar boys in the next room before turning to issue final instructions to his team.

'When we go out on to the altar we'll genuflect two by two and then go round the back and kiss the altar. There's chairs at both sides for you to sit in.'

There was a solemn silence while the sacristan checked that lights and sound were turned on – son et lumière as the Parish Priest called it – and having communicated his intentions, it appeared, by some form of telepathy to the choir outside, he opened the door, and to the strains of 'Hail Queen of Heaven' they processed solemnly out into the church.

It was the golden jubilee of the Little Flower Novena Society, and as one-time spiritual directors of that august body they had been invited to concelebrate the jubilee Mass – or, as the invitation had phrased it, 'to participate in the concelebration of the Eucharistic Liturgy'. It was an invitation not lightly to be refused, for the Society's internal intelligence service was known and feared throughout the diocese, and only genuine alibis could hope to withstand their scrutiny. The leading lights in the organisation were a pair of pre-Vatican II stalwarts who viewed all ecclesiastical change as a victory for the Communist party and regarded the Spanish Inquisition as one of the Church's better ideas. They were seated in the front row, looking like a pair of Indian chiefs who had just won the battle of the Little Bighorn and were planning an encore. Behind them sat the rest of the tribe, equally unamused, but slightly less fanatical. They had not sold out to the opposition, but they valued public opinion, and, now that they had accepted such soul-shattering novelties as lay-readers and offertory processions, they were confident that no one could accuse them of dragging their feet in the liturgical renewal.

The leading concelebrants reached the centre of the altar – and kept going. Only the presence of a battle-hardened altar boy prevented them from continuing straight out of the sanctuary and into the graveyard. The Parish Priest, who was bringing up the rear, eventually reached the centre of the altar and genuflected, with six concelebrants on his right and none on his left. He led the way round to the back of the altar and kissed it and they all duly followed him in a single line, but they now found themselves marooned in the centre of the sanctuary with nothing to indicate which side they should go to in order to sit down, so they weaved in and out for a while like a troupe of superannuated Irish dancers and more by luck than by design eventually finished up three on each side.

This shaky start unnerved everyone so much that by the time Joe was due to do his first reading he failed to notice that an intruder – lay and female – had already entered the sanctuary and was heading for the lectern with obviously the same intention as himself. He had his own ideas about canonical precedence, but there was no way he was going to tackle a heavyweight matron wearing clothes like a wartime bridesmaid, which she had obviously bought for the occasion, so he admitted defeat and shuffled back to this chair, mentally contemplating what to say to the Parish Priest when the show was over.

Needless to say, having observed this debacle at close range, Billy was not going to make the same mistake, so when it came time for the responsorial psalm Billy sat tight and waited. The expected reserve team from the congregation never appeared, and eventually what might have passed for a brief period of silent prayer grew less brief and more silent until Billy was finally persuaded that the opposition was not going to show and he might safely do his stuff. He headed for the lectern in determined fashion, as if defying anyone to stand between him and his allotted task, and this time no one did; but as so often in the affairs of men while the initial blows of fate may be avoided, fate usually has another spanner up its sleeve. The microphone was fitted to the end of a springy gooseneck affair for the average cleric; in this case a foot higher than Billy could cope with. In fact, even the lectern hid most of him, except a shiny dome bordered by tufts of spiky grey hair, so before starting he reached up and pulled the microphone down to his own height and then launched himself into the responsorial psalm. His basso profundo voice, of which he was inordinately proud, rang through the Church with a pleasing echo, but then started to fade into nothingness as the microphone took on a life of its own and rose slowly back to its original position. Billy quickly slammed it down into place again and tried another time but no amount of vocal projection could compete with the relentless diminuendo of the device. With every line he sounded more and more like Stan Freberg's recording of the 'Banana Boat Song'. However, he persevered valiantly to the bitter end, and then struggled back to his seat, looking like a contender for the title who had just survived fifteen rounds and lost all of them.

Jamie had viewed his colleague's embarrassment with complete equanimity, indeed with a certain amount of amusement, for he knew that he would have no such trouble with the second reading – always assuming, of course, that no further saboteurs were launched from the body of the Church – for he stood six-foot-two in his socks and towered high above most difficulties. Murphy's Law, however, had obviously swung into action at the start of the service and there seemed no reason for it to throw in the towel at this stage.

Jamie ran his eye over the lectionary, looking for St Paul's observations on men who had wives and instead found himself eye to eye with a wide selection of texts on death and dying, for

Billy had forgotten to turn back the pages after his defeat by 'The Lord is my Shepherd'. Jamie was not sure which way to go. Was it the common of virgins he was looking for, or of holy women, or of religious, and were they backwards or forwards from his present position? In a less stressful moment he would have homed in on the text without difficulty, but now he panicked and started rippling through the pages backwards and forwards in the vain hope of catching a lucky glimpse of St Paul. Needless to say he found his fill of St Paul – and St James and St Peter and St John too – but none of them was the text he was looking for, and he was still no wiser about whether to turn forward or back or stay where he was. He stood for a while, *nihil dicens*, as they say, and then he licked his thumb and started leafing through the pages one by one, and with every page his head bowed lower and lower over the lectern.

It was probably the thought of what Jamie's wet thumb was doing to his precious lectionary that galvanised the Parish Priest into action, for he swooped like a buzzard on the lectionary, grabbed a red marker tab that had somehow evaded Jamie's notice and slammed the book open at the right page. Jamie stumbled through the reading, anxious only to get it over and done with, and then slunk back to his seat to join the ranks of the vanquished.

The Parish Priest had figured it was time to stamp his authority on the proceedings before things got completely out of hand, so he read the gospel with a crisp emphasis and afterwards delivered a few ponderous but dependable clinches on the role of the saints in the eternal plan of salvation. He then stepped back to the altar and was about to launch into the offertory when Nemesis overtook him too, this time in the shape of the commander-in-chief of the Little Flower Novena Society and his trusty adjutant, who both approached the lectern carrying a sheet of paper apiece in their hands and obviously intent on revealing their contents to the congregation. The Prayers of the Faithful! The Parish Priest had completely forgotten about them. So totally indeed had he forgotten them that he had prepared neither introduction nor final prayer, and now he could only mumble 'The Prayers of the Faithful' and stand silently while the duly appointed representatives of the faithful said their prayers and departed. Fortunately, this moment of crisis jolted him into awareness that there was an offertory procession as well, so he was able to mobilise a couple of far-from-enthusiastic auxiliaries and do the needful without completely revealing his oversight to the assembled brethren

It was reasonable to assume at this stage that the fates had done their worst and nothing further could sabotage the remaining operations – at least in a way that could seriously compete with what had gone before. But this was an unwarranted assumption. As the concelebrants were sitting quietly in their seats, observing the prescribed moments of silent prayer after the Communion, yet another figure starting to approach the altar, but this time not only the clergy but even the seasoned veterans of the Little Flower Novena Society were caught on the hop.

It was a rotund, bearded gentleman, wearing filthy clothes, with a woolly cap pulled down low over his ears, and he was only too familiar to the entire congregation, lay and clerical alike. William McCloskey, better known as Willie the Wino, the last man on earth to be overcome by the solemnity of any occasion. While his feet may have refused to take accurate instructions and meandered first to one side of the aisle and then to the other, his eye remained fixed all the time like the ancient mariner on one of the concelebrants.

'It's wee Fa'er Pillock!' he announced at the top of his voice, and even the staunchest of clerical supporters in the congregation had to hid a grin, for Jamie's Anglo-Saxon surname of Pollock had been the subject of many humorous variations during his term as curate in the parish.

'Is that you, Fa'er Pillock? I haven't seen you for years. How're ya doin', Fa'er?'

Never had Jamie regretted so much all the pounds he had contributed over the years to Willie the Wino's upkeep. That a man's sins should come back to haunt him was understandable, if regrettable, but that his goodness of heart and largesse should pillory him before the public gaze was surely the ultimate injustice. He sighed deeply, put his elbows on his knees and rested his head in his hands. 'This too shall pass,' he told himself, but he was not entirely convinced.

It took a little time to recruit a suitable team of bouncers from the Little Flower Novena Society, but Willie was eventually escorted off the premises and the Parish Priest wasted no time in winding up the proceedings. He blessed the assembled brethren in the name of the Father, Son and Holy Spirit and told them to go in peace, and while the choir sang 'Faith of our Fathers' they all shuffled back into the sacristy, regardless any longer of order, precedence or decorum.

There was an uneasy silence as they took off their vestments and they avoided any direct eye contact. This state of affairs continued for some time until finally a disembodied voice from the ranks muttered hoarsely, 'It's a good job they don't have a jubilee every year.' And with that the ice was broken, peace was restored and they all went away happy.

*'F***!' screamed the Parish Priest.*

Letter to a Young Priest from his Uncle, A Senior Priest

Dear Nephew,

I found myself sitting near your parish priest at dinner, following a recent clerical funeral, and as you know, nothing tends to lighten the spirit and loosen the tongue like the death of a colleague. Perhaps it is relief at having avoided his fate, or perhaps the joyful anticipation of filling his shoes.

At any rate, your pastor, or to give him his proper title, of which he is so inordinately proud – the Canon – on that occasion held forth at length on the vicissitudes of clerical life and especially the daunting responsibilities of a parish priest in this age of *aggiornamento*, all of which I would normally have allowed to flow past me without comment had I not at one point in his oration heard him mention your own name.

It was not done in any spirit of complaint or criticism, but rather with that air of desperation which characterises a drowning man who finds that the log to which he had been clinging is in fact a crocodile. It would appear that the generation gap, which heretofore he had maintained in reasonable proportion, has suddenly widened since your arrival in the parish into a yawning chasm that threatens to engulf him.

I could not but sympathise with the man in his agony. I had experienced a similar culture shock some years back when the Bishop sent me a young man whose obvious intention was to change the world – eventually – but in the meantime, for want of a wider canvas, he was content to begin with myself and the parish. We both survived the ordeal – myself and the parish, I mean – but I carry the scars to this day, so in the hope of sparing both yourself and the Canon a similar fate, may I address a few words of avuncular guidance to you across the arches of the years.

Your pastor belongs, like myself, to a generation that was trained in the virtues of obedience and conformity. One was not encouraged to question the wisdom of superiors – indeed to do so was to be branded 'singular' and deemed guilty of a 'grave irregularity'. But even in that age of innocence the Canon was a noticeably innocent man. Far from exploring the emotional life of the clerical neophyte and pushing out the boundaries of self-consciousness he was what one might call the negative embodiment of the Cartesian maxim *Cogito, ergo sum* ('I think, therefore I am.'). With him it rang something like 'I am, therefore I do not need to think!'

He obeyed the rules, or avoided detection – in his eyes much the same thing – and found adequate fulfilment in the occasional pat on the head from his superiors for being a 'sound' man. (The pat was strictly metaphorical. Any hint of a physical pat, on the head or elsewhere, from anyone, especially his superiors, would have been viewed with grave suspicion. His highly developed sensitivity – if not allergy – to any form of sexual ambivalence tended to prejudge the most innocent gesture and was known on occasion to lead to strong language and even physical violence.)

Imagine his consternation then, when, in the course of his daily constitutional around the town he recently came face to face with yourself through the window of the local unisex parlour, not merely having your hair permed, but having it done in full view of the public gaze by a mini-skirted young lady of obviously frivolous disposition. (I merely paraphrase his report.)

I know that by now there is a surfeit of clerical heads in the diocese that have been dyed, shaped, permed and blow-dried and I am sure that the Canon knows it too, but I have the feeling that he fondly imagines that, far from patronising female hair salons, the afflicted clergy creep furtively on their day off to some ring-poled barbershop of dubious reputation in a mean backstreet of the city for permanent waves or other such effete embellishments. That his curate on whom he depends to inspire the young men of the parish with manly Christian virtues should submit to such effeminate adornments, and invite public observation of the spectacle, has introduced a new and unpredictable element into his favourite doctrine of 'muscular Christianity'.

In similar vein your ultra-modernistic fashion in lay-clothing would seem to be causing him some anxiety. It is not that he is unaware of today's tendency to don civilian clothing occasionally but somewhere in his subconscious is the belief that a mature and responsible priest will not exceed the traditional sports shirt and grey socks with which his contemporaries naively strive to conceal their Levitical status. Your appearance about the Church in white training shoes, monstrous yellow jacket, and a pair of tight-fitting jeans that have been ripped and slashed in the most alarming places (I will spare you his robust description of this garment, though I should mention his wonder that you did not ask the housekeeper 'to put a couple of stitches in them'!) him considerably, especially when you ventured into the confessional wearing them.

Already the repercussions are being felt. One pious lady has approached him with the unique moral *casus*, 'If you get bad thoughts when you are confessing your bad thoughts, is it better not to confess the original bad thoughts at all?' A question which I fear, elicited a response more notable for its chauvinism than for rational analysis. It might be argued that the causative link between your attire and her dilemma is not proven, but in the Canon's theological perspective to be even the occasion of such disorder is a mortal offence.

While we are on a sacramental theme may I say that it was daring, if not foolhardy, of you to sweep all the Canon's private notes and memoranda from the altar into a collection basket ('like a bloody head-waiter clearing tables') prior to celebrating your Sunday Mass, but it was quite catastrophic of you not to return said notes and memoranda to the altar before the Canon celebrated his Mass. The resulting confusion – if popular report is to be believed – culminated in the Canon praying for the happy repose of several members of his hall committee and reading the Prayers of the

Faithful from the Marriage Ceremony – these being the only prayers he could lay hands on at short notice. Such insensitivity has, I fear, introduced a highly emotional element into the situation which may prove immune to the curative powers of reason.

Several other aspects of your Eucharistic celebration came in for fairly trenchant criticism.

I would be the first to agree that music is a most apt concomitant of public worship, but do you really think that a solo performance of 'The Joys of Love' to your own guitar accompaniment from the presidential chair was a suitable alternative to the responsorial psalm?

Might I also question the wisdom of introducing an element of dialogue into your homily by asking the congregation what they thought the modern priest should be working at in his parish. Apart from the fact that they must surely wonder that you did not learn the answer to this fundamental question in the course of your seven long years of training, it is always worth keeping in mind that ancient caveat regarding prayer of petition. 'Be careful what you ask for. You may not like the answer.'

Your exhortation to the congregation at the sign of peace 'to give each other a good squeeze' was likewise ill-advised. Apart from the fact that even for some of the married couples in your congregation such behaviour could well be an innovation, it is worth remembering that, a few brief years ago your predecessors and mine were beating these same people from the highways and byways with blackthorn sticks for indulging in precisely the same behaviour as you are now advocating from the altar. That some of them will still regard it as matter for Confession is beyond doubt, but there are even a few pious mothers who, as they view their innocent brood alongside them, will regard it as nothing short of an incitement to incest.

Many other areas of pastoral activity were touched upon, but I will not continue to heap burning coals upon your head.

The central theme of my message is, I hope, clear. (Incidentally, I am reasonably certain that your pastor's fear that you intend to introduce liturgical dance into the Sunday liturgy will prove groundless, but should the question arise I must, *ex cautela*, forewarn you of the perils of such an undertaking. You might mistakenly envisage some tasteful *pas de deux* executed by slender dancers in diaphanous robes, but I have personally seen the local handmaidens of Terpsichore in action on a previous occasion and let me tell you that even fully clothed they are not a pretty sight. Enthusiasm is no substitute for expertise, and on that occasion the enthusiasm of the performers was only surpassed by the embarrassment of the spectators.)

May I suggest that you endeavour to lead, rather than drive, your pastor into the mysteries of the twenty-first century. You will recall the ancient Irish belief that the insane and the feeble-minded enjoy the special protection of divine providence. Well, the privilege is also, in my experience, extended to parish priest, of limited intelligence and imagination.

Your esteemed pastor is one of that happy band of brothers. He always escapes the retribution to come as I will endeavour to prove to you with a few brief but carefully chosen illustrations.

You may have heard that before administering the sacrament of Confirmation in days of old it was the custom of the Bishop to select random candidates for examination in the tenets of the faith, and to subject them to personal scrutiny at the altar rails. At such times pastors tended to bite their nails in fretfulness and pray for deliverance from the far side of some suitable pillar. The Canon, however, merely wandered around the church exchanging pleasantries with all and sundry, and on one occasion was so oblivious of the growing tension at the altar rails that when the Bishop, in final exasperation, called out to him, 'Canon, these children know nothing,' he merely replied, 'Is that a fact M'Lord; and you have the pick of them up there.'

You may also recall that it was the custom for the Sisters of Nazareth to visit each church annually while a collection was taken up for their work of caring for orphaned and abandoned children. While some innocent Sister accompanied the collector around the church on Sunday morning the Canon called loudly from the altar. 'And you boys standing at the back, mind you give plenty, for it is your youngsters they are looking after.'

For neither of these comment was he subjected to even one word of criticism.

You may also have heard of the unforgettable occasion when a bridesmaid turned up at a marriage in his church wearing a sleeveless dress. The young lady had travelled from Scotland, and was not aware of his obsession with female modesty. He managed to restrain himself during the opening prayers but his searing glare in her direction every time he addressed the congregation gave warning of turmoil to come. He finally burst the chains of discretions and snarled at a nearby altar boy, 'Bring me a surplice.' When the terrified messenger returned with the garment he merely pointed at the transgressor and ordered, 'Tell her to put it on.'

Once again he escaped retribution; this time because the young lady in question assumed that this was merely one of the more exotic rituals of the Irish marriage ceremony.

Even his more-than-Gothic ignorance of the ways of the world is pardoned without comment, as witness his suggestion that the problems of the local disco could be solved by having one night for boys and another night for girls.

May I caution, therefore, against the use of shock tactics in your dealings with him. Victory is always possible, but a pyrrhic victory is merely another name for defeat. Your more nimble intelligence will, I am sure, find ways to smooth the path of collaboration. Remember that the devil you know is preferable to the devil you do not know; and should you rashly disregard this oft-quoted but undeniable pearl of wisdom you may discover by the hard road of experience that there is a profusion of much tougher, smarter and meaner devils scattered around the diocese.

Your ageing uncle.

Wedding of the Year

The Canon paced up and down the sacristy like a nervous sheep. Already he was regretting his decision to allow the bride's American cousin to concelebrate.

He had stoutly resisted the intimidations of her mother, a lady with the build of a Sherman tank and a personality to match, but he had crumpled before the blandishments of the bride, a petite young lady with a coaxing smile and a wealth of experience who had returned home for the wedding after six years in the city and who had learned all there was to know about getting men – especially older men – to do what she wanted.

'I'd much rather have you doing my wedding, Canon, but you know what my mother is like. She would hate to miss a chance of showing off her nephew. But don't you worry. He'll just stand alongside you and give you no bother.'

The Canon was not so sure. He had checked up on this clerical migrant and discovered that he was a Professor of Pastoral Sociology – whatever that was – at some nameless American University, and if there was one subspecies of the human race that made the Canon nervous, it was 'intellectuals'.

He rearranged the vestments, scolded the altar boys, pattered out on to the altar and moved the candlesticks a third of an inch to the left – for the fourth time – and looked meaningfully towards the door of the church. It was now fifteen minutes past the hour and there was still no sign of the bride. He called down to the first row of guests.

'Is there no sign of her yet?' but the level of sound produced by the spotty-faced youth at the organ – who was giving an adagio performance of 'You By My Side', which the Canon mistook for the 'O Salutaris' – was drowning out all conversation, and when the Canon enquired a second time and merely got a cupped hand-to-ear from a mystified guest, he raised his voice in a crescendo of irritability and screamed, 'Will you stop that squawking and squealing up there. I can't hear myself think.'

The spotty-faced youth stopped his performance, and with a gesture of true artistic temperament, slammed the lid of the organ down with such violence that it sent a shockwave through the entire congregation. The Canon was sorely tempted to pursue the argument, but with the accusing eyes of the guests all focused on him, he decided to cut his losses, and shuffled angrily back into the sacristy, just in time to meet his American rival for the hearts and minds of his parishioners.

He hated him from the first moment. Not only was this interloper tall, well-groomed and confident, but he carried a black leather briefcase with a combination lock, the ultimate status symbol of the upwardly mobile cleric. In the Canon's book, you could warm to a man who carried his alb in a plastic bag, but the briefcase brigade aroused his deepest suspicions. They might not carry the badge of office in their lapels – yet – but they definitely worked out of head office.

He opted for a cold and formal approach. 'Good morning, Father. I am Canon Charles Kenmore, Parish Priest of Castlegorm.'

The visitor looked him over for a moment, and then responded in a similar vein. 'Good morning, Canon. I am Monsignor Jeremy Cromwell, Professor of Pastoral Sociology at the University of St Polycarp and visiting Professor to the Catholic University of America,' and just as the Canon had got as far as asking 'Are you …?' he added, 'and I am *not* related by birth or marriage to the Lord Protector.'

From that point onwards the declaration of war was taken as read, and battle was joined.

'We are simple country people here, Father,' announced the Canon. 'We do not go in for gimmicks or novelties in the liturgy.'

'How wise of you, Father,' replied the Monsignor. 'It will be quite time enough, I am sure, to modernise your liturgies when you have to contend with such manifestations of modernity as colour television and the singing tavern.'

Since the parish was liberally dotted with both these innovations, and since he had frequently lambasted both of them from the altar, the Canon had to suffer in silence. Obviously, someone had squealed. He eyed the Monsignor grimly.

As they donned their armour, a glacial silence prevailed. The Monsignor scored a further point by dropping to his knees on the only prie-dieu in the sacristy and bowing his head in silent prayer. The Canon was well aware of the importance attached to such practices by retreat masters and spiritual directors, and had always excused himself on the grounds that if he did not see to the preparations for Mass himself they would not be done properly, but now he unaccountably found his defences wilting. He leaned over the vesting bench in an attitude of reverential piety, put his head in his hands, and plotted how to pull this turkey-cock off his perch.

When word came of the bride's arrival they both bowed solemnly to the cross, and the Canon waited pointedly while the Monsignor, in his role as assistant celebrant, led the way onto the altar. They genuflected together, and then, to the Canon's consternation, instead of going to the rear of the altar to await the bride, as was customary, the Monsignor turned on his heel and walked confidently down the nave to the front door of the church. It was done with such panache that the altar boys followed him without hesitation, and the Canon, finding himself abandoned halfway up the altar steps, had no choice but to follow.

At the door, the Monsignor greeted the bride with a most un-clerical embrace and complimented her rapturously on her choice of dress, her hairstyle and the general radiance of her appearance, so that when the Canon finally got her attention there was little more that he could add. He passed himself with an awkward handshake, and turned to lead the procession back up the church, but once again he was out-manoeuvred, for the Monsignor stepped smartly in front of him and led the way back up the church in his flamboyant American chasuble, smiling and nodding like royalty, in time to the music, and completely blotting out the Canon who came shuffling behind.

As the congregation settled down for the start of Mass, the Canon's temper was still boiling, and he vowed solemnly that there would be no further infringements of his rights and privileges as principal celebrant, but his vigilance was unnecessary. The visitor behaved like a lamb. He meekly took his seat to the side of the altar and at the appointed time approached the ambo and read the lesson in a relaxed if somewhat over-modulated tone of voice. The passage was unfamiliar to the Canon; from the Song of Songs perhaps, or some of the less familiar chapters of Isaiah, he wondered. The Monsignor then gave way gracefully to him and the Canon duly read the gospel and afterwards launched into his famous dissertation on the erosion of traditional family values and the urgency of a return to the simple lifestyle of their parents and grandparents. When he had finished – twenty minutes later – he moved straight to the bride and groom without any signal whatever to his concelebrant and began to read the preliminary address of the marriage ceremony. The American, however, was in no way put out. He merely slid into place on his right as the Canon got to the core of the proceedings.

'John, will you take …?'

'Jason,' whispered the Monsignor in his ear. 'His name is Jason.'

'What?' barked the Canon. 'What did you say?'

'Jason. His name is Jason,' replied the Monsignor in a stage whisper that reached the back of the church.

'Oh,' muttered the Canon. 'Right. James, then. James, will you take—'

'Jason,' shouted the Monsignor. 'The groom's name is Jason.'

The Canon looked at him in disbelief.

'Jason? His name's Jason?' he queried.

'Yes. Jason. J-A-S-O-N. Jason.' Spelt out the Monsignor.

'Jason! Jason!' repeated the Canon. He was sorely tempted to question the likelihood that anyone could have been christened Jason, but he resisted and ploughed manfully on.

'Jason, will you take …?'

It upset his rhythm for the rest of the ceremony. He lost the page, dropped the rings and spilt holy water all over his precious new carpet.

He finished the wedding ceremony with a sigh of relief and turned back towards the altar, but the Monsignor stopped him in his tracks with a crisp announcement.

'You may now kiss the bride.'

The Canon looked at him in amazement, and then suddenly realised that the instruction was not addressed to himself, for the bride and groom were by now exchanging a long, lingering kiss in which they were strongly encouraged by the broad smiles and loud applause of the Monsignor and the assembled guests.

The Canon had never witnessed an exhibition like it in all his life; and his horizons were further widened when the Monsignor himself stepped forward and kissed the bride on the lips, and embraced the groom like a presidential candidate soliciting votes. The Canon was too stunned even to protest. He offered the bride and groom another awkward handshake and trailed miserably back to the ambo thinking thoughts of vengeance and violent death for the Monsignor.

As he ploughed bravely on through the Mass, the Canon's mind kept wandering to the ubiquitous American and how he might anticipate his next outrageous attempt to hog the limelight. No one, he told himself grimly, was going to turn the liturgy in his church into a three-ring circus, and so intense was his concentration on the Monsignor that he allowed the musicians to slip under his guard with a soulful rendering of 'Annie's Song' during the offertory, something that would normally have been stopped dead in its tracks.

He was reasonably confident that he could sabotage any further departures from strict liturgical practice, but his mind kept jumping ahead to the sign of peace. It was not that he was against the sign of peace as such – though he had considerable reservations about the wisdom of the practice – but the thought of calling the peace of the Lord down on the American in his present state of mind troubled the Canon's scrupulous soul; and yet, not to do so would draw the displeasure of the entire congregation down upon him. He nobly resolved to bury the hatchet and try to face his God and the Monsignor with as clear a conscience as possible.

However, even such a massive surrender of principle on his part did nothing to avert the slings and arrows of outrageous fortune, for as he called upon the congregation to offer one another the sign of peace, he saw the Monsignor out of the corner of his eye heading towards the bride and groom without so much as a glance in his direction.

His good intentions withered on the air, and once again he found himself trailing in the Monsignor's wake and offering the bride and groom the same awkward handshake that by now had lost all semblance of meaning, while the Monsignor passed on down into the congregation and offered kisses and handshakes and embraces to everyone from the groom's mother to the man driving the bridal limousine. How long it would have gone on there was no telling, but as soon as the Canon got back to the altar he called out 'Lamb of God' in such malevolent tone of voice that even the most dedicated bestower of peace got the message and called a halt to the revelry.

No further calamities befell the Canon during the remainder of the Mass and he duly herded his team into the sacristy, while the bride and groom paraded behind him to the strains of 'God Bless This Couple Who Marry Today'. He contented himself with overseeing the registration of the marriage – visiting clergy tended, in his experience, to regard the Signing of the Register as an optional extra – and was about to retire gracefully to the presbytery for a much-needed cup of tea when the bride insisted that he should have his photograph taken with herself and the groom and the little flower girl. The latter was a diminutive young lady whose head was barely visible above the registration table, so the Canon, in a most untypical burst of goodwill, picked her up in his arms and directed his usual tortured grimace, which served as a smile, towards the camera. This unexpected gesture of benevolence won the enthusiastic approval of all present, and the Canon departed for his cup of tea feeling pleasantly elated, for it seemed to him that he had stolen a march on the Monsignor and proved that where the fundamental virtues of compassion and sensitivity were concerned, he had not been found wanting.

The Canon had intended to time his arrival at the reception to coincide with the end of the first course. He liked to encourage the belief that he was a man who was busy about his Father's business; he also liked to make an imposing entrance while the others were seated at table. Unfortunately, his timing was badly off on this occasion, and he arrived just in time to join a long queue of guests who were slowly making their way into the dining hall to the tune of 'Congratulations' on the hotel public address system. Their creeping rate of advance puzzled him considerably, until he reached the door of the Dining Hall and found the bridesmaids, the groomsmen, the bride's mother, the groom's mother and father and the bride and groom all lined up to shake hands with the guests as they entered, and at the end of the line, clad now in a white polo-neck sweater and showering hugs and kisses upon the ladies and clutchingly sincere handshakes upon the men, the bumptious American Monsignor. By now the Canon's handshake was as limp as a dishcloth, and it was only by a supreme act of will that he was able to extend his hands to the Monsignor and mutter through clenched teeth, 'I see we meet again, Father.'

He passed into the Dining Hall and was immediately commandeered by an effeminate young man with a napkin over his arm who addressed him as 'Sir' and led him to his place at the end of the top table. The Canon's mood was far from sociable as he sat down and it was not improved by the arrival beside him of the groom's father – a brash, overweight talker, with a tankard of beer in his pudgy fist, who greeted him with rude familiarity.

'Well, Canon, how's it going? That's a grand big priest you had helping you with the wedding. No oul' show or nonsense about him.'

The Canon cringed at this salutation and tried to think of a suitably abrasive response, but before he could answer he was almost lifted out of his skin by the crack of a long-handled serving spoon hitting the table beside his left ear.

'Reverend Sirs, ladies and gentlemen,' called out the young man with the napkin. 'Pray, be upstanding for the bride and groom.'

The Canon was still shaking with fright as he struggled to his feet, but he courteously joined in the applause as the bride and groom and the little flower girl made their smiling way to the top table, and he was gently easing himself back into his chair when he was lifted into the air once again by another explosion to his left, while the prissy young man called out, 'The Reverend Monsignor Cornball will now say grace.'

The Canon guffawed heartily at this mistake, but his merriment faded rapidly to crimson embarrassment as he realised that everyone else in the room was looking at him in stony-faced silence. The Monsignor's fulsome blessing upon the food, upon the cooks and upon those about to eat it did nothing to improve his spirits, and neither did the wearisome commentary of his neighbour on all the 'grand' priests he had met throughout the diocese, most of whom the Canon regarded as little short of clerical beatniks. However, he was well used to the meanderings of semi-intoxicated wedding guests, so he merely responded with his usual selection of non-commital grunts and nods. Meanwhile, he hacked his way through the inevitable chicken and ham dinner, and was vainly trying to identify the ingredients of what passed for sherry trifle when the ubiquitous young waiter crept up on his blind side and lifted him out of his chair once again by whacking the table with his long-handled serving spoon. A volley of rifle shots, fired from close range, would have done his nervous system less damage.

'Reverend Sirs, ladies and gentlemen, pray silence for the Best Man'.

The Best Man, in the honoured tradition of his tribe, had all the command of language and syntax of a sick parrot, and contented himself with mumbling, 'The bride and groom will now cut the cake.'

The Canon applauded politely along with the other guests, and then stiffened as he saw the Monsignor rise with a sheaf of telegrams in his hand and a smile on his face that boded no good for the weak and the restless. He read the greetings – including the obligatory marital jokes – with reckless gusto, and followed them up with a lengthy speech that owed more to the Official Irish Joke Book than it did to the Sacred Scriptures.

He was followed by the uncle of the bride, the groom's father and then the groom himself, and only a timely elbow in the ribs from the bride reminded the Best Man to call upon the Canon to say a few words. By this time the Canon's store of patience and charity had run out, and he rose to his feet in a fit of peevishness and launched into a diatribe of denunciation that included immoral films, 'bad' television programmes, pornographic books, godless communism, rock and roll (the more recent music innovations had not yet come to his attention), dimly lit discos, fruit machines, liberation theology, and the pitiful quality of the rising generation of clergy. He then went on to castigate the shamelessness of modern dancing and the chronic abuse of alcohol in the parish, before finally addressing himself to the bride and groom, whom he contrasted for modesty and decorum with some of the current models in his parish, before finally calling down upon them some obscure Irish Blessing which wished them freedom from unjust landlords and a generous price for their livestock at the next market.

The applause was dutiful rather than heartening.

In the fading twilight the Canon limped home exhausted to be met in the doorway by a chuckling Senior Curate. 'How are you, Canon? I hear you've been promoting the heathen scriptures and giving your blessing to trial marriages.'

The Canon snarled back at him. 'What are you talking about? I'm in no mood for your juvenile humour.'

'Did you not hear the lesson yer man read today? It was straight from the Koran. And that pair you married today, they've been living together up in Dublin for the past five years. Who do you think owned the youngster they had with them?'

An angry ball of fire exploded in the Canon's head as he realised the extent of his naivety, and he planned long and lingering tortures for all concerned. Suddenly, the colour drained from his face and the anger departed. The photograph! Himself and the child and that deceiving pair of … They wouldn't surely put it in …

But they did. The following week, the local newspaper carried front page coverage of the wedding. Under a photograph of the Canon, with the little flower girl in his arms and the happy couple by his side, was the caption 'Wedding of the Year'.

'… the Canon … directed his usual tortured
grimace … toward the camera …'

The Cardinal Myth

Ask any reporter – television, radio or print – to outline the command structure of the Catholic Church and the chances are he will get it wrong. These men know the labyrinthine workings of European Commissions; they can explain NATO and the United Nations and tell you who can vote for what and when; they can even keep track of Northern Ireland political parties and their paramilitary supporters; but they cannot tell us who runs the Catholic Church. They know about the Pope, but after that they are lost. They insist on portraying cardinals as important people.

In reality, cardinals are nobodies. If you know someone with the title of cardinal who, in your estimation, is a 'somebody' it is because he was successful in some other field of endeavour before he became a cardinal. The fact that he is a cardinal now is merely confirmation that he was successful and influential before he became a cardinal.

Cardinals, in fact, have no authority and only two privileges. They are the senior advisors to the Pope – if he chooses to listen to them – and they have the right to cast a vote in the election of a new Pope – if they are under eighty. Otherwise, they have no authority whatsoever.

The appointment of Bishop Connell as cardinal has highlighted this anomaly. Sean Brady is Primate of All Ireland – whatever that means – and he will remain primate even if every other bishop in the country is made up to cardinal. His primacy stands on a completely different foundation altogether and is unaffected by any proliferation of cardinals.

The only office wielding any authority whatever in the Catholic Church is that of bishop. Forget about archbishops, auxiliary bishops and even coadjutor bishops – though these last do eventually step into power. In the day-to-day running of the church bishops have all the muscle. If you are a bishop of a particular place such as Armagh or Dublin it does give you an extra title but it gives you no right to interfere with the running of another diocese. The bishop is the boss of his own diocese. That is the most basic truth of the command structure within the Catholic Church.

There is one exception. Priests who belong to a religious order – and some nuns – are not subject to the authority of the local bishop. Their chain of command runs from the local superior – that is the man or woman in charge of the local house or monastery – to the superior general or what Rome now calls the supreme moderator – the person in charge of the entire religious order.

When Fr Brendan Smith was eventually called to account for his crimes, many reporters asked, 'Why did Cardinal Daly not step in and ban this priest from holding office where he might have contact with children?' And the answer is very simple. He had no authority over Fr Smith. Only Fr Smith's superior – because he belonged to a religious order – had authority to tell him where he might or might not operate. After all, you do not expect an admiral of the fleet to give orders to a private in the paratroopers. Of course, if he were on loan to a particular diocese and misbehaved in any way the bishop has the right to ask his superior to recall him, but the bishop's power over him is indirect. As long as he remains a member of a religious order only his superior – in this case his abbot – has authority to tell him to come or go. Cardinals do not come into the picture at all.

And what about archbishops? Surely they have authority over the bishops in their province? Again the answer is no. An archbishop has no authority to interfere in the affairs of another diocese unless the Pope authorises him and that is a very rare occurrence. Even archbishops with titles like 'Primate of All Ireland' gain no authority by the title. The Code of Canon Law, which is the rulebook of the Catholic Church, says quite bluntly 'The title does not carry with it any power of governance.' (The only responsibility devolving on primates is to inform on their fellow bishops to Rome when they step out of line!)

The sad, but little-known, fact is that the title of cardinal gives no one any extra power except, as I said, the right to vote in papal elections and give advice to the Pope if he asks for it. They get to dress up in fancy robes but the title gives them no authority – though it probably does give them a certain amount of influence without responsibility – and you know what Stanley Baldwin said about 'influence without responsibility'.

However, all is not lost. There is one area of life in the Catholic Church where the title of cardinal may even yet play an important part. All kinds of people have been cardinals in their time. Popes have frequently given the title to their nephews, and Julius III even gave it to a fifteen-year-old lad he picked off the streets of Parma, and while the bystanders might not have all approved, no one suggested that the Pope had exceeded his authority. A cardinal does not need to be a priest or a bishop or an archbishop or even a deacon. It would seem that no qualifications are necessary for the job, so here is what I suggest.

Let the Pope call another consistory and there let him announce the names of another batch of cardinals, only this time they will all be women. Whatever about women priests and the theological disputes surrounding them, there is no theological or canonical impediment to the appointment of women cardinals that cannot be removed with the stroke of a pen. And if the Pope has any difficulty coming up with names, just let me know and I will be happy to supply a few candidates. He has been unloading redundant monsignors and time-serving technocrats on to the Irish Church for a good while now so this is our chance to hit back with a few colourful candidates of our own. After all, Christ did say 'I have come, not to bring peace, but a sword!'

Clerical Characters

Every time a group of clergymen come together, some senior member will inevitably bemoan the disappearance of all the clerical characters he used to know. The younger members will probably be too polite to point out that, while he doesn't know it, he is now one of those characters. Not perhaps the unique, unforgettable character that used to grace the pages of Reader's Digest, but a more routine, common or garden variety. The very fact that he has survived so long entitles him to membership of the club, but he will probably only qualify on grounds of a single quirk of character, rather than by virtue of his whole personality.

The standard or regular clerical character is likely to be remembered, for example, for his scathing tongue. The man who listened to an old lady boasting that she was eighty-five years of age and then commented 'Imagine that now. And cartridges only twenty pence a piece,' is a typical example. Or maybe he is one of the hot-tempered fraternity, ready to invite any critic out to the street, or maybe he is the aspiring orator whose accent changes to Oxford blue as soon as he mounts a pulpit.

These are the lowest grade of character and they usually make little impact on posterity. On a slightly higher level are the do-it-yourself and hobbies experts. They're not as common as they used to be, because everything, from fruit to furniture, is more available nowadays, and probably cheaper to buy than it is to make. It wasn't their expertise in these fields that won them renown, but rather their more obvious mistakes or shortcomings. One man, who is lovingly remembered in this district, liked to do minor repairs about the house. He eventually aspired to greater things and decided to convert his attic into a bedroom. All day long he could be heard hammering away merrily until the last board was laid and the last nail driven home, and then there was what the novelists describe as a 'pregnant silence', followed by the sound of floorboards being furiously ripped up again. He had become so engrossed in his work that he boarded himself into the attic and left no way out.

All of these, however, are merely pale reflections of the real or genuine character, one of whom it was my privilege – and my penance – to know and work with. He had all the marks of his profession to a unique degree – supreme indifference to public opinion, a complete lack of respect for any authority but his own, sufficient years to be untouchable by superiors, indifference to the ups and downs of the human condition, and the necessary health to be able to enjoy it all.

He had a reputation for holiness, but if you live long enough this is fairly easy to acquire. He spoke as if he were perpetually contending with a badly fitting set of false teeth – which he probably was – snapping them together at the end of each word to prevent them shooting across the floor. He had once written an article for a theological magazine, back in 1923, of which he was inordinately proud, and he continued to make sporadic attacks on the field of creative writing, but he typed, as one curate said, the way he spoke, and both were equally unintelligible.

He slept anywhere at anytime, as the inclination took him, but most of the night was spent wandering restlessly about the house.

On one occasion he went to attend an old friend who was ill and was duly escorted into the sick room, but when two hours had passed and he had not reappeared the lady of the house grew alarmed and went upstairs to see if anything had happened to him. At first glance she could see nothing in the room but the patient sleeping peacefully, but on further investigation discovered the missing clergyman on the far side of the bed, flat out on the floor, and also fast asleep.

Every morning, whether he had slept or not, he came waltzing down the stairs – no other word can describe his progress –

swinging from the stair-rail with one hand and carrying in the other hand his own brand of *sine qua non*, a white enamel bucket. This was not a good time to be standing at the foot of the stairs, as the bathroom was on the ground floor and accidents did occasionally happen.

He regarded the parish as his own private playground and any games that were missing he soon installed on his own initiative. He believed firmly in the good old days and the good old ways of doing things. Occasionally he would announce a concert in the parish hall. No mention was ever made of performers, but when the audience had all finally gathered in, he would mount the stage and call on members of the audience to come up and sing or recite or display whatever other talents they possessed.

Sunday mornings were often better than any concert. His timekeeping was erratic, because he insisted on giving twenty minutes grace to people from the hills. His congregation, however, were well used to this because his predecessor was even more erratic, and one old man was heard to remark, the first morning he appeared in their midst, a mere twenty minutes behind time, 'God be with good old Father so and so. Barring you came on a Monday morning you couldn't be late for Sunday Mass.' He preached when and as the spirit moved him. Even such a straightforward task as reading out the priest's collection, in accordance with ancient custom, took on a new twist. He added a running commentary, so that the final result sounded something like this: 'John Smith: half a crown. Are you sure you can manage it?' 'William Jones: ten shillings. I thought the sheep would have paid better than that, Willie.' 'Patrick White: three pounds. Now there's a man knows the price of coal.' While Patrick, in the third row down, blushed furiously.

He was generous to a fault, reaching into the collection box and giving large handfuls of coins to the altar boys because it was a good day and they might be going to the seaside. He also gave money to people who had no need, or even desire, for it, forcing it on them with unshakeable insistence simply because he liked them. He liked to 'treat' his church workers at Christmas, so every Christmas morning a large bottle of whiskey was produced and those who hadn't taken to their heels early enough were dragooned into the sacristy for their Christmas drink. The last time I witnessed this ceremony he had a slight problem. He had forgotten to bring glasses. But he was not to be defeated. When I returned to the sacristy all hands were standing around, red faced, while they toasted in the Yuletide season from variously shaped flower-vases.

It's doubtful if he ever acknowledged anyone as a figure of authority, but if he did they were all long since dead and gone, so he was free to live his life unruffled by lawful superiors. A foolhardy bishop once attempted to bring him to heel, with disastrous results. He merely assured the bishop in the most condescending manner that he was still a young man, and had much to learn. The only effect of this, however, was to leave the bishop purple with rage, but he just patted him on the head and repeated, 'Jesus meek and humble of heart.'

Where his own authority was concerned, however, he gave no quarter. Occasionally, strong-minded individuals – but more usually timid individuals driven to desperation – rose up in rebellion, but he invariably subdued even the toughest by dropping to his knees and imploring the Almighty at the top of his voice to spare this misguided sinner from the vengeance they so thoroughly deserved. I can tell you – from personal experience – that this kind of tactic was quite intimidating.

His control over his congregation was absolute. On one occasion he was warned that the gallery in his outlying church was dangerous – indeed that it was liable to collapse without warning if immediate repairs were not carried out. This suggestion – that something old might be somehow defective – touched a sore point, so on Sunday morning when Mass was finished he told the women and children to leave and then ordered all the men into the gallery. 'Now,' he said, 'when I say jump, I want everyone to jump.' And jump they did – not over the gallery, but up and down and thus was it proved to his complete satisfaction that however old the gallery, it was still safe for generations to come. The possibility of wiping out the generation on the spot in one fell swoop never seems to have crossed his mind.

Right to the end of his days he maintained his independence and his eccentricity. It was his custom to spend the summer holidays in a run-down house on the coast of Donegal where he passed the time sleeping, swimming and talking. As he approached ninety his doctor declared the sea out of bounds, and gave him a stiff lecture on the possibilities of heart attack or pneumonia, but he might as well have saved his breath. He continued to take his daily dip in the ocean, attired in his 1930 style bathing suit, and returned slapping his chest and holding forth on the beneficial effects of cold water. His housekeeper was finally forced to confiscate the bathing suit, despite strong objections, but he eventually gave way and retired, in apparent defeat, to his bedroom, but she might have known better. He borrowed her scissors later in the day and locked himself in his room. Next morning he appeared, dressed in home-made bathing trunks, which he had concocted from a spare bath towel and a few strategically placed safety pins.

Next year, all bathing attire, old and new, was confiscated and the scissors were put under lock and key, but even then he was not to be outdone. How he outwitted her she didn't learn until later in the day. A genteel English couple who were holidaying nearby called at the house because they were worried, they said, about 'the old gentleman'. Apparently they had been taking a quiet stroll on the beach when this apparition arose like Venus from the waves and went streaking past them, naked as the day he was born, muttering to himself, 'That'll show them, that'll show them.'

And show them he did – not alone his amazing ninety-year-old physique, but his intense freedom of spirit. He refused to be classified or numbered. He refused to be regimented or organised. He merely insisted on his God-given right to enjoy the journey through life, and if he so wished, to travel it by a route that no other human being had yet explored.

April Fool

The publication today of the long-awaited report from the Vatican on 'Clerical Celibacy and Associated Matters' has taken both critics and commentators completely by surprise. Those who were expecting another vaguely worded compromise – and very few were not – have had to eat their words, because the message has come back to them loud and clear, that from 1 July next, clerical celibacy will no longer be compulsory, and that women will be admitted to the Catholic Priesthood.

What this will do to the holiday schedules of some parishes, one shudders to think, but more urgent issues are facing not merely the Irish bishops but a lot of parish priests as well. The purely logistical problem of accommodating this incursion of clerical spouses is bad enough, had priests merely been permitted to marry – and the experts forecast that anything up to fifty per cent can be expected to take up their option of marrying in the first six months – but the further complication of simultaneously admitting women priests – who will, no doubt, in their turn, also want to marry – means that community parochial houses, those former bastions of male domination and unquestioned authority, may soon become the battleground for a fight to the death between clerical husbands and un-clerical wives on the one hand, and un-clerical husbands and clerical wives on the other.

The more positive commentators have pointed out that at least parish priests will be spared the burden of deciding upon the rights and privileges of clerical children, at least for the present, but the more cynical have suggested that we may see a very rapid reappraisal of the Church's stance on matters such as birth control, with the central issues of condoms and contraception fading discreetly into the background before very long.

However, even the Vatican has foreseen that the new order may experience some teething problems before it gets finally bedded down – if you will pardon the expression – and so they have added a few clauses and conditions that may help to curb the worst excesses of the initial onslaught. Parish priests have been given a right of veto on their curate's choice of partner – somewhat like the Security Council of the United Nations – which at least ensures that the parish priest's worst nightmares will not come to life, but does nothing to ensure that his fondest dreams of peace, privacy and protocol will be maintained.

The document does indeed lay down the protocol to be observed on liturgical occasions, even specifying that the priest's wife should be addressed as 'Madam Priestess' and that she is entitled to occupy a special chair within the sanctuary while her husband is saying Mass, but it makes no effort to establish any order of precedence or privilege on the domestic front. As for peace and privacy, even the Vatican knows that a crying baby – or worse still, several crying babies – write their own laws, and will ultimately do what no curate has ever dared to do and play havoc with pastor's hitherto carefully guarded sleeping patterns.

Reaction to the document has been varied. That was to be expected, but the intensity of emotion which it has aroused, among both defenders and attackers, has given warning of troubled times to come. From a random sample taken this morning, comments have ranged from the baleful warning of a senior parish priest, 'Over my dead body,' to the plaintive cry of a middle-aged curate, 'Now they change it. They had to wait until *now*.'

As was to be expected the introduction of woman priests has caused far more bitterness among senior clergy than the introduction of clerical wives. Subconsciously, at least, the term 'wife' still implies subordination, so on this front their nerve is holding, but the idea of woman priests not merely attacks the final stronghold of male domination, but it now seems likely to carry the war right into the enemy's sitting room and his kitchen.

One thing is certain; the old order has passed away. The best we can hope for is a life of quiet desperation; the worst a life of chaotic frustration. Myself, I think we are in for the worst.

Middle Age

This is a desperate plea on behalf of middle age.

Actually, it is more like Custer's last stand, for already the defenders of middle age are badly out-numbered and ammunition is running dangerously low.

Since time began, youth and old age have held centre stage. They have been celebrated and congratulated as though to be young or to be old were in itself some kind of personal achievement, when in fact middle age is the only stretch of existence when we confront life with no excuses.

When you are young you are hampered by the antiquated attitudes of parents and other fossilised figures of authority, so you can't be blamed for the mess the world is in. When you are old you can only bemoan the present state of the world and tell us what you would have done if you had had our easy money and golden opportunities in those days long ago. When you are middle aged you are too busy trying to keep a roof over both their heads and your sanity into the bargain to say anything.

For the record, let it be said that I do not stand outside the issue, giving a calm and impartial judgement about it. I am involved to the very hilt, and I have a very real personal stake in restoring middle age to its rightful place among the ages of man.

middle age is not determined by any kind of mathematical calculation. It is a purely visual thing. In other words, you are only middle aged if you look middle aged. If you have a full head of hair, a well-preserved figure, and your own teeth, then it does not matter what age you are. On the other hand, if you are bald and have rounded shoulders and a wobbly stomach, then it does not matter if you are only nineteen, you are still middle aged. There is no sort of logic or rationality to it. You merely look at someone and you see baggy trousers and a jacket that is straining around the armpits and you say 'middle age'. Premature perhaps, but middle age nonetheless.

This means of course that some fortunate people never see middle age. They pass from youth to old age in one graceful flowing movement. The rest of us, however, have to live with it as best we can and that is where the trouble starts, for there is enormous pressure on us either to conceal it or delay it.

A vast international conspiracy has been hatched to abolish middle age, engineered by the television industry and financed by the cosmetic and the health-and-leisure business. It started in the late fifties when teenagers were first invented. Up until then there had been children and adults – young adults and old adults – but that was it. We had to wait for the television age before this new race of humans was discovered. The commercial world badly needed new markets for its superfluous luxuries so it created a new world, a fantastic dream-world where pleasure was a basic civil right and responsibility was a dirty word.

It caught on like wildfire, because it embodied the ambitions of every dreamer – rights without responsibilities, and pleasure without pain. Television, ever faithful to the mathematical calculation of success, counted heads, and not merely bowed its own head before the invading hordes but got down on one knee and adored them. Suddenly there was a revolution in the television business, and a lot of seasoned practitioners found themselves out on the street, relegated in a day from the position of public personality to membership of the dole queue.

In a business where you could be forgotten if you went to the toilet, people began to have serious doubts about their own existence, their careers vanished so quickly. The wise and humble realistically took to their heels and fled underground before the mob could catch up with them, hoping to come back and fight another day. The foolish stayed to fight it out and were routed in a tidal wave of mimicry and contempt. The swingers took over.

Overnight the staid and respectable realism of middle age gave way to the irrepressible optimism and eternal smiles of the new messiahs. Hardened political veterans were grilled by these youthful interrogators and cut down in mid-sentence because they wanted to explain. Dedicated musicians and singers were shown the door because they insisted on hitting the note, neither above it nor below it.

Patched jeans and a granny shirts became the official uniform of television producers. Outdoors, worn sheepskin coats and climbing boots were compulsory. Behind the cameras, baldness was no impediment; in fact, it could be a bonus if it was set off with a droopy moustache and long sideburns, but in front of the cameras any indication of biological wear and tear, such as wrinkles or fat, was sacrilegious, and offenders were punished with immediate and everlasting excommunication. Newscasters were the only exception. An image of solid reliability was essential for the news, so they were grudgingly allowed to stay on.

All of this helped to create an image of middle age as a socially unacceptable condition. By excluding it from everything that smacked of fun, freedom and happiness, the conspirators gradually conditioned us to reject it as something akin to bad breath or haemorrhoids. You didn't talk about it in polite company and you avoided contact with it if at all possible. In fact, we soon developed the same kind of embarrassment and resentment about it that young people have about sickness and old age. If you have ever seen the film *The Effect of Gamma Rays on Man-in-the-Moon Marigold*, you will remember the older child's hysterical reaction to the old woman who came to board with them. Well, we have all been trained to react in the same way to middle age, unless of course we have already contracted the disease, in which case our family and friends try to keep us out of sight, like consumption cases in days gone by, and steer the conversation rapidly away from any enquiries about our health or our present whereabouts.

This policy has driven us all like sheep into the arms of the health and appearance experts, exactly as it was intended to, and conned us into spending our last reserves of energy and money in the hopeless attempt to stem the approach of middle age. Why else do you think we all go running marathons or joining Unislim or buying outrageously expensive books about what Jane Fonda is eating or not eating to keep her figure trim. Do not try to pretend that it has something to do with health. That is just another camouflage that we have been encouraged to hide under. If we were really worried about our health we would have stopped smoking years ago – without anyone telling us – and we would have cut down on our drinking, and that is only after we had deserted the fumes and pollution of the city and gone to live on some mountaintop; but we all know that we would be bored out of our skulls in a week if we took our health seriously so we indulge ourselves to the hilt until the warning signs of middle age suddenly appear, and then we start back-pedalling furiously in a desperate struggle to keep it at bay at least for another year or two.

If it has already arrived, then we have to take a different approach, but here too we get plenty of encouragement and all the equipment necessary to conceal the bad news. In fact, the amount of stuff on the market for the sole purpose of concealing middle age defies imagination. Take a walk around the cosmetic counters in any pharmacy and you will see what I mean.

Even the medical profession seems to have joined this campaign to mutilate middle age. They have conditioned us to believe that this is a time of life when the body itself starts acting strangely so we ought to expect heart attacks, high or low blood pressure, depression and such things as a matter of course. I disagree entirely with this view of life. I see all these calamities as the inevitable consequence of our emotional neglect and deprivation. Like the traveller in O. Henry's story 'The Roads of Destiny', no matter what path we follow, we end up being shot by the same bullet.

The ambitious young man pursues power. He sacrifices family, friends, loyalties, in fact everything that might impede him in the furious climb to the top of the pyramid. At forty-five he has nowhere to go except down. The result: depression.

The serious-minded young man wears himself out providing for his family. At forty-five they have all flown the nest, impatient to begin their downward journey into oblivion. The result: depression.

All roads lead to the same destination – middle age depression. Nothing can prevent it. But the world could help us to survive it, and it does not. The merest suggestion that we even exist might help. A word of encouragement would do wonders to lift our spirits, and a gesture of congratulations would leave us floating like a cloud.

Somehow we are fated to be both the indispensable nucleus of the human race and at the same time the forgotten age.

I missed out on my teens, for teenagers had not been invented. I am missing out on middle age because someone has abolished it. With my luck, if I ever survive to old age, euthanasia will be compulsory, and some little man will be waiting round the corner with his syringe, ready to cheat me out of my third and final chance of enjoying the best years of my life.

The Pictures

Occasionally, a layman whom I am meeting for the first time will launch into a discussion of the latest papal pronouncements or the theological opinions of Edward Schillebeeckx – this apparently being considered a suitable kind of conversation for clergymen – when, in fact, we would both probably feel much more comfortable with some normal subject, such as the weather, or Manchester United if we are really stuck. And that is why I intend to bypass all the serious stuff and to confine myself to something simple – if not frivolous.

Way back when I was young – in the pre-television era – the great popular recreation, apart from the more obvious indoor sports, was going to the cinema, or the pictures, as they were then called. For us children it served as an incentive for good behaviour and a sort of reward for services rendered, and the thought of getting to the pictures on a Saturday afternoon gave a whole new meaning and purpose to the rest of the week. One did not – at least in our house – just decide to go to the pictures. You had to ask if you could go, and when you had satisfied my mother that the particular film in question would not constitute any danger to your emotional or moral well-being you were given a provisional approval on condition that you did not blot your copybook in the meantime.

Getting this approval was not always easy because my mother had an intense suspicion of the film industry in general – stemming, I suspect, from some of the more flamboyant Cecil B. DeMille productions which she had seen in her younger days in

Glasgow and which stood forever after as a typical example of the loose moral tone and dubious behaviour that pervaded the entire film industry. We found it useful then, when we were seeking permission to go to the pictures, first of all to insist that the quality of films had improved vastly since those days, and also to present the film of our choice as a western – no matter what the subject matter might be – on the widely held assumption that westerns dealt only with the punishment of evildoers – the 'baddies', and since most of the time on-screen was spent by both parties in pursuing one another over the prairies in endless chases it was assumed that they would have little opportunity, and less time, for indulging in any kind of immoral hanky-panky with the ladies. The worst that could occur was a chaste kiss for the heroine in the final reel, and even that was regarded by the experts in the front stalls as a completely unnecessary waste of valuable action time.

We hit upon a scheme, one time, for convincing my mother that the movie business was now as pure as the driven snow – in the hope that it would smooth our path when we next went looking for permission to go to the pictures. We would choose a particularly harmless film – preferably a western – and take my mother with us to see it. Having seen with her own eyes the completely innocuous nature of the modern cinema she would henceforth have no hesitation in allowing us to see all the films we wanted. However, as Robbie Burns so aptly put it, 'The best laid schemes of mice and men …'

My brother was entrusted with the task of choosing a suitably harmless film for her to view, and, come the night in question, and after much eloquent persuasion – for my mother had not set foot in a cinema in the intervening twenty years – we all set out for the pictures, confident that from now on we had it made. The first intimation of disaster came when we got to the door of the cinema and I saw this gaudy poster advertising a completely different film. There was a hurried council of war between myself and the brother, and while I stalled my mother he hurried off to do a quick check on the programme. When he returned his face was more eloquent than any words. 'I got the dates wrong,' he said. 'It is not coming until next week.'

There was no going back, however, at this stage. We were well and truly cornered, for our thesis had been from the start that the entire industry had changed for the better and that there was no such thing nowadays as a film that would bring a blush even to the cheeks of your maiden aunt. We could not have been more wrong. Right now, I cannot remember what the name or even the subject matter of the film was, but from our point of view it was a disaster movie of epic proportions. There were randy sailors climbing in and out of bedrooms – and beds as well – and there were hysterical ladies rushing about in various states of undress screaming to be rescued. We just sat frozen to the seats – mentally and emotionally pole-axed – and implored the Almighty to bring it to a close as soon as possible.

That night's work set my cinematic expertise back about two years. It was only when time had healed the wounds and we had persuaded my mother to venture into a cinema once again – this time to a carefully checked and vetted western – that she was willing to acknowledge that the entire film industry was not rotten to the core.

It was only right and proper that the good old western should have been our salvation. After all, that was what westerns were all about – the ultimate victory of good over evil, against fearful odds. The western hero was all that doting mothers wanted their sons to be – brave, honest, courteous – he invariably lifted his Stetson to ladies and called them 'ma-am' – but above all he was honourable. He always let the other guy go for his gun first – and then blew the head off him. He was a straight shooter, in every possible sense.

However, as the years passed, the cracks began to appear in these plaster saints of the silver screen. Making due allowance for the cynicism of youth, I was still fairly devoted to my heroes when someone gave me a book called *The History of the Wild West*. What I read there shattered the very foundations of my western faith. Billy the Kid, it appears, was not the fearless foe of all baddies. He was a murderous young psychopath from the back streets of New York, and Doc Holliday of O.K. Corral fame was not a gambling gunslinger with ice in his blood, but an alcoholic dentist who drank himself to death. And there were other longstanding heroes whose good name took a hammering at the impartial hand of history.

No matter. Even if a few idols had fallen by the wayside there were still the nameless heroes of the western way of life – the sheriffs, the Texas Rangers, and, of course, the Seventh Cavalry, riding to the rescue in the nick of time. Legend might have misled us about the talents of our darling sons, but the lifestyle, the whole western philosophy, it was still the same.

Well, for a long time, at least in my mind, it was, but last year, quite by chance, it was shattered into such tiny pieces that I doubt it will even recover. I found an old book, covered in dust and obviously untouched for generations, and when I had cleaned it up a little I settled down for a quick look through it. *Missionary Adventures in Texas and Mexico* by the Abbé Emmanuel Domenech. Not exactly the kind of title to get the adrenalin going. However, as I poked my way through it I suddenly realised that the time (1845–51), the place (Texas) and the man (an impartial foreigner with first-hand experience) were all just right for an accurate account of the Wild West.

The results could not have been worse. Listen to what he says about his local sheriff:

> Were those that deserved it most brought to the gallows, the very hangman would be first, followed by a goodly number of judges, barristers and doctors, headed by the sheriff himself. He was a man of immense stature. He carried at this waist a six barrel revolver and in his hand a cow-hide lash, making frequent use of both. His expressionless features bore the impression of cruelty.

And as if this was not bad enough the man was also a coward, for even the poor Abbé Emmanuel was able to stick a gun in his chest and frighten the boots off of him.

And what about the Texas Rangers – those fearless defenders of the right? 'They are the very dregs of society and the most degraded of human creatures,' he says. 'These bloodthirsty men, who have neither faith nor moral feeling, massacred a whole division of the Lipan Tribe who were quietly encamped near Castroville; they slew all; neither woman nor child was spared.'

And the United States Cavalry? Well, this is where it really went to pieces.

> In isolated camps, soldiers were at the mercy of their commanders, who feel or entertain a deep rooted, innate hatred for Irishmen. The most barbarous chastisements are inflicted. I have seen soldiers suspended by the arms from the branches of trees for drunkenness. Sometimes they tie their arms and legs and fling them repeatedly into a river, and then drag them back to the bank with a rope.

The full story is too long to be told here, but it deserves to be told. In it all my boyhood heroes bite the dust, and the only survivor with any kind of honour is the Indian – and he was supposed to be the baddie. But then, of course, they have started making movie heroes of the Indians too, so I suppose it is only a matter of time before someone finds another book and the redskin comes toppling from his perch like all the heroes before him.

Letter Writing

My letter-writing career never really got off the ground until I went to St Columb's College as a boarder in the late 1940s. Prior to that my literary efforts were confined to a few infantile expressions of gratitude to my maiden aunt for her hospitality – whether indeed I had enjoyed it or not. Coming to St Columb's, however, meant that letter writing had to take on a completely new meaning and purpose, for it was no longer a question of throwing together a few cliché-ridden expressions of thanks and licking the envelope on them, but of pouring out my soul with a passionate intensity that would soften the heart of my mother and persuade her to come to my rescue.

Let me explain things – for those of you who were not boarders in St Columb's College in the late forties. For those of you who, like myself, were boarders during that forgotten era no explanation is necessary. The beginning and the end of all our activities, the alpha and omega of all our schemes, was the acquisition of food. Everything was directed to that purpose and nothing took priority over it for we were perpetually hungry. I realise now, of course, that there wasn't a great deal that the college authorities could do about it for the war had just ended and everything was scarce – indeed, some things were still rationed – and the problem was compounded by the ravenous appetite that all growing boys are afflicted with. Their hunger just didn't fit into any normal scheme of things. What was considered adequate for an adult appetite didn't fill us, so we always left the table hungry, and since there were no recreation rooms or places where we could sit down and rest we either kept walking 'round and 'round the grounds like caged animals, or else kicked a tennis ball around the gravelled football pitch, and in doing so worked up a colossal appetite which, of course, was not satisfied at the next meal, and so we walked some more and played some more football and so on.

Just to give you an idea of how ravenously hungry we were, let me digress a little further. 'Tea' in those days, consisted of tea, a slice and a half of bread and two pats of butter. Breakfast consisted of tea, a slice and a half of bread and one pat of butter, so the more enterprising students saved a little of the butter from teatime and stuck it to the underside edge of the table with a knife to supplement the rations at breakfast-time. This was considered a fairly ingenious and far-seeing tactic because, in theory at least, the stash was hidden from view and wouldn't be disturbed by the kitchen staff when cleaning the table. However, like the concentration camps I've read about since, it wasn't the guards you had to look out for so much as the other prisoners. Come breakfast time, an even more enterprising student would get to the table before anyone else and with his finger hooked under the edge would slide it the length of the table and scoop up the butter ration of anyone foolish enough to have left it there.

Faced with this kind of struggle for survival, we had to supplement our diet, or perish in the attempt, and that was where letter writing came into its own. The man who could write his parents a good letter, one that presented an appealing mixture of rugged determination and childish pathos, would see it bear fruit in the form of food parcels, or, just as acceptable, money to buy food. So you set yourself to write a letter that would pluck at your mother's heartstrings. (You quickly learned that fathers did not send food parcels. At best they might part with some money, but even then mothers usually had to effect the separation.)

Now for someone with no previous experience of this kind of moral blackmail it wasn't easy to master all the technical details, like, what do you call your mother in a letter? Dear Madam? The English teacher had told you that you should begin a letter 'Dear Sir or Madam', but he was talking about writing to the Inspector of Taxes or the editor of *The Times*, and it didn't seem likely to help your case if you began with the usual commercial jargon 're yours of the 14 inst., I beg to inform you'. On the other hand this was a boys' school and a boarding school to boot, and heaven help you if you showed any signs of weakness. Sissies and softies had to be rooted out, and anyone who started his letters 'Dear Mammy' was at least suspect, if not guilty, of girlishness. You mightn't go so far as to refer to her as your 'old lady', but you were expected to adopt a suitably macho attitude when addressing mothers and other such relics of your childhood, or alternatively, to keep your correspondence well hidden. I kept mine hidden, and with my head bent over the desk and my left arm protectively curved around the page I penned the first words of this masterpiece of power and persuasion: 'Dear Mammy.'

At this point the words should have come tumbling out in a torrent of eloquence, depicting in all its horror the grim life that I was now living, but somehow the creative flow seemed to dry up. I found myself struggling for something to say, something that would undoubtedly catch her attention but which would not create the impression of an overgrown baby in a state of pitiful hysteria. I knew instinctively then, and experience has since confirmed it, that if the first sentence of a letter doesn't grab you the chances are that the rest of it will not even get the chance.

I've always admired those letter-writers who could get straight to the heart of things, without any preamble or introduction. I think the most effective example of it I have come across was a letter from a man called George. His wife arrived on my doorstep one Christmas morning, tears tripping her, and this letter clutched in her hand. It was short, succinct and straight to the jugular. 'Dear Sarah, I want nothing more to do with you, George.'

Children, too, seem to have developed this skill to a high degree. When they write a letter there is no messing about with formalities or explanations. 'Dear God, OK, I kept my half of the deal. Now, where's the bike?' Or, 'Dear Santa Claus, I want two baby brothers for Christmas, one smaller and one bigger than me.'

Bishops, too, used to have the knack of writing a letter that hit you between the eyes like a loaded cosh. 'Dear Fr Collins, I am sending you as curate to Ardstraw West. Please arrange to be in your new place for Saturday.' This kind of communication, arriving out of the blue on a Monday morning, was guaranteed to make you sit up and pay attention, especially since you hadn't been expecting it for another five years. The shock of the transfer, and the realisation that he wasn't kidding about next Saturday, ensured that you read and reread the letter until the contents were branded forever on your memory.

Letters from bank managers and tax inspectors should, by all the laws of logic, have a similar effect, but in practice they merely terrify the recipient. He is more likely to read just the first line, and then drop in his tracks from a heart attack. I had a friend who was so terrified of official letters, especially those accompanied by a sheaf of unintelligible government forms, that he ceased to open any of his mail, no matter how harmless. He took the whole lot – official letters, Christmas cards, birthday greetings from his mother, even refunds from the taxman – and cast them all into a small room and closed the door on them. I think he had some wildly irrational idea that if he could keep it up for long enough they would all eventually go away. Needless to say, a day of reckoning finally arrived, but even then he couldn't muster up the courage to face the consequences. He appointed a proxy to deal with the chaos – and for three weeks I had the exhilarating experience of roaming freely through another man's correspondence without any of the usual feelings of guilt. I may say that, on balance, I think he should have faced the music earlier, for apart from the official letters and documents there was a grand total of £1,200 in cash and cheques in it as well.

However, I'm straying very far afield, and this article is rapidly taking on the shape and pattern of my letters in those far-off days. My original intention was to do a sweeping survey of the whole art of letter writing. There would be learned quotations from Thomas Bodleigh and Archbishop Usher, a passing reference to Madame de Sévigné, a dip into the Viceroy's postbag, a few words of spiritual uplift from de Foucauld's *Letters from the Desert*, – did you know that he wrote 734 letters from the desert to his cousin alone? – and even a word from the devil himself in *The Screwtape Letters*. I intended talking about begging letters, anonymous letters, problem letters, love letters, chain letters, Dear John letters, letters to the newspapers, fictional letters, even letters about letters – the kind that Eric Gill used to enthuse about – but instead what have I composed? Another highly personalised ragbag of trivialities and that's exactly how my school letters used to go. The noble intentions gave way to the routine miseries of life and the necessity of filling a few pages. They were never as long as this, but they were just as banal. 'Dear Mammy, I hope you are well. We played football on Saturday. Our team won. I have to study Algebra. It is very difficult. I must finish now. Your loving son, Michael. PS Please send a parcel and some more money.'

Even the memory of them is embarrassing, but I have an even greater fear than the memory of these past indiscretions. My mother is a most economic woman. She saves everything. Even the most useless and worn out items are tucked away in the bottom drawer, in case they come in useful some day. I have nightmares that somewhere among the debris are my pathetic letters, and that years from now some bargain hunter will discover them and I will be remembered forever by the very things that I would most like to forget.

The Troubles

Stragglers in the Night

In the course of a clerical life it may be your misfortune to be housed in accommodation that has been designed by a parish priest. If so, you have my deepest sympathy. Mercifully, this is a rare occurrence today, but occasionally a would-be cathedral builder will slip through the net and design a cross between a cattle shed and an aircraft hanger for a presbytery. It was my misfortune to be housed in one of these structures where the priest–designer had based his vision of the future on the plentiful supply of priests available at the time, whereas on this particular night I was the sole resident of the eighteen-room barrack which he had dreamed up.

It was built to the same plan as the aforesaid cattle shed – long walkways with rooms opening out to the right and left but with variations that only the clerical lifestyle could account for. At each end of the corridors there was a staircase, one for the priests and one for the housekeepers. God forbid that some innocent curate should meet an aging female in her dressing gown and curlers on her way to bed. Who knew what lascivious thoughts she might foment in his innocent mind. And since priests might not stray into housekeeping territory without a signed affidavit that they were of sound mind and body and no danger to the inhabitants, the toilet facilities at their own end of the corridor were of a type normally found in commercial premises only – a double stall, where you could attend to the calls of nature and discuss the political situation in Outer Mongolia with your neighbour at the same time. It was not a well-designed house.

At 2.30 a.m. the doorbell rang with a grating persistency and as usual I struggled into my well-worn dressing gown and shuffled, first to the staircase, then down the stairs, then along the corridor and finally to the front door, where the bell was still ringing loud and clear. I wiped the sleep from my eyes and after some effort finally unlocked the front door.

'You weren't in your bed were you Father?' On the doorstep stood a fairly seasoned supporter of the alcohol business and behind him – to paraphrase the late Damon Runyon – his ever-loving girlfriend.

'You weren't in your bed were you Father? I hope I didn't waken you.'

I directed a long, chilly and pointed gaze at him, indicating at least a moderate degree of dissatisfaction, but he continued unabashed. 'Would you ever give meself and the girlfriend a lift to Shantallow?'

'Would I what?' I asked in disbelief.

'Would you ever give us a lift to Shantallow?'

'Why can't you take a bus to Shantallow? And if the buses have all gone couldn't you take a taxi?'

'Ah Father there's that much trouble and crime nowadays that the buses close down before dark, and the taxis are so afraid of being hijacked that they all pack it in before one o'clock. The last taxi I was in the driver told me he was robbed only the night before by three young fellas with masks and guns.'

'And why do you think I'll be safe in the road with all this criminality going on?'

'Ah sure they would never hijack the priest. You'll be as safe as houses Father.'

The discussion continued in this vein for another fifteen minutes and I began to realise that my only hope of getting these late-night revellers off my doorstep was to get them to Shantallow and leave the residents there to deal with them.

'Stay here,' I said. 'I'll be back in a minute.'

Getting them loaded into the car was not the simple operation I had envisaged. The girlfriend, Faustina, who was well under the weather, wanted to sit in the passenger's seat, whereas her escort Sean Seamus wanted her in the back. Eventually I felt called upon to pronounce judgement, like the prophet Daniel, and I told her to get into the back unless she wanted to walk to Shantallow.

The first roadblock was down by the Quay and the little squaddie on duty looked at me suspiciously and asked 'Got any identification, maite?' I duly produced the driving licence and he looked at it. 'Rev. M. Collins Adm. Adm.? You some kind of a bishop or what, maite?'

'No. I'm a lowly priest just inches above the lowliest level of churchman. If I were in the army I'd be a lance corporal.'

'Don't knock it, maite. It's better than being a f******g private. On you go.'

I had solemnly warned the passengers that if they opened their mouths at the checkpoint I would personally borrow the soldier's gun and shoot both of them and then drive over their inert corpses, and they had paid due attention to my warning, but as soon as we cleared the checkpoint they launched into a strident tirade of vilification and profanity about Her Majesty's Forces and their lack of respect for the clergy. They continued to assert their disapproval of occupying forces in a loud and raucous manner, but it was only as I approached Shantallow that I realised that an element of conflict had now entered their discussion and Sean Seamus and Faustina were going at one another hammer and tongs about whether or not the little squaddie at the checkpoint was 'cute' or otherwise. Needless to say, Faustina was supporting the squaddie and Sean Seamus was asserting his intense disapproval of any suggestion that a member of the British Army, the perennial enemy of all true republicanism, the oppressor of the Irish nation down the centuries, could in any circumstances be described as cute.

In due course I reached my destination, and politely asked them to remove themselves from my car and let me get home to bed.

Whatever they had been drinking, however, had obviously begun to take effect at this point, and I had to resort to some loud and violent language to try to persuade them to get out of my car and let me go home, but I might as well have been talking Greek.

Sean Seamus urged me to hold on for a minute while he explained the historical background of his heartfelt opposition to all aspects of the British Army, while Faustina explained to him in fairly trenchant language that he was a 'stupid s**t who wouldn't know the difference between a good-looking man and a pile of manure'.

It took threats of violence and even the suggestion of ecclesiastical penalties to finally move them from my car but eventually they moved out. I turned and headed for home and stopped only for the little squaddie who was still maintaining his lonely vigil along the Quay. I said to him, 'If you only knew the time of it I've had tonight listening to an argument about whether you are cute or not.'

His face lit up. 'My mum will be pleased to hear that. She always thought I was cute.'

Three in the Morning

It was three o'clock in the morning and, as I struggled into consciousness, it seemed to me that I had been wakened by a loud unfamiliar banging noise coming from the front of the house. I could not identify it, so I sat up in bed and waited to hear if the performance would recommence, and sure enough the banging started once again from the same direction, followed by the furious ringing of the front door bell.

Some of my colleagues will insist on getting fully dressed before answering the door bell in the middle of the night. Myself, I just struggle into a worn-out dressing gown and stagger down the stairs hoping, pessimistically, that there will be some tiny iota, some minute trace, of reason and sanity behind this disturbance.

Sadly, there rarely is, and in this instance the opening scene did not give much promise for a happy finale. Standing on the doorstep, or more accurately, leaning against the door frame, was a one-legged, highly intoxicated Scotsman, who proclaimed to the world in a hiccupy voice his total dissatisfaction with the revolutionary violence around him and with current Church thinking on the theology of the just war. And he indicated his intention of here and now making his own unique contribution towards a resolution of both these timeless dilemmas.

I took him into the waiting room and sat him down, and for half an hour he lectured me on the Church, the clergy, the sad decline in public morality and his general unhappiness with the state of the world. And just as I was about to pull down the curtain on his meandering monologue I remembered the banging noise. Had he heard this? 'Aye, that was me, I was banging on the windy with me crutch. I could nae find the doorbell.' This merely reinforced my determination to call a halt to his performance so I informed him that the interview was now terminated and I was going back to my bed since, unlike himself, I had to get up in the morning. He disagreed strongly with this line of reasoning but I insisted that enough was enough and he had to go; with this proviso, that if he wished to call at a more reasonable time, preferably in daylight hours, I would be happy to accommodate him. He obviously expected a better service, but he finally departed, under duress, and I went back to bed.

I had barely wrapped the sheets around my weary body before the banging noise started up again. Only this time it was even more noisy. I endured the turmoil for about a minute but eventually I had to rise and investigate. Once more I donned the trusty dressing gown and headed for the front door which I slammed open without waiting for any invitation from the doorbell or the knocker and standing in the middle of the car parking area I found my one legged Scotsman balancing himself on his useful leg and throwing the crutch that served as his substitute leg at the window of the parochial office. I called upon him to desist. In fact, I called him a 'stupid f*****g bastard' and told him that if he did not desist I would use his crutch to assault him with such violence and such precision that his eyes would water for a long time to come.

I might as well have been speaking in Greek. He continued to launch his crutch like an Olympic javelin at the office window and dared anyone to come between him and his chosen target. I had no alternative but to come to close quarters and deprive him of his offensive weapon, and that, I assumed, would be an end to the proceedings. It just showed my naivety in these matters. As I turned to throw away the offending crutch he hopped energetically towards my car, which was parked at the doorstep, and anchored himself to the passenger door while he launched the remaining crutch at the innocent office window. I had no alternative but to confiscate the offending crutch, leaving him to cling in frustration to the car while he described my origins and my likely destination in the afterworld in colourful words of one syllable. I tried negotiating a truce that would allow both him and me to get back to bed before morning but he was immune to all forms of diplomacy or mediation.

I was about to give in and return his crutches when a small boy, about ten or eleven years of age, peeped around the corner of the gatepost, obviously looking for someone but in a manner that distinctly lacked enthusiasm. I knew there had to be some connection between him and the Scotsman so I ordered him in a loud and menacing voice to step forward and identify himself. 'That's me da,' he said. 'I've come tae take him hame.' His explanation was mercifully brief and his accent largely incomprehensible but it would appear that his da had gone on a drinking spree and had failed to materialise in the family home at the appointed hour, so following a well-worn routine his ma had sent him first to the pub to check if he was still drinking and if he were not to go to the nearest parochial house since the churches were all closed at that hour, and if he could not be found at the first house to move on and spread the net a bit wider until he was found. This was all told in a very matter-of-fact style and when I raised the question 'What if your da does not want to go home?' He merely smiled and said nothing. He gathered up the crutches, propped them under his father's arms and said, 'Right, let's go.' And without a word of objection or complaint his father, following what seemed to be a well-practised routine, fell into line in front of his tiny son and headed silently for home.

Eventually I returned to bed, but sleep was impossible. My world was turning upside down. Parents were reckless and irresponsible and children were left to pick up the pieces. Maybe I had lost touch with reality. Maybe this was considered normal behaviour. Maybe I should have taken up a different line of work.

Con

It was the early days of the Troubles. Parents still expected the school bus to run according to schedule even while hijackings and bomb scares were creating havoc on the roads.

The bishop was regarded as all-powerful so if you had a complaint that needed answering or a defect that needed repair you went to the bishop. And he took care of it. Of course, someone else had to take care of it for no bishop could possibly have attended to all the problems that came crowding across his doorstep during what were euphemistically called the Troubles. The bishop passed the problem down the line to the parish priest or the administrator as he was called in Derry City, and the administrator passed the problem on to the curate, the man who handled all the problems.

On this occasion the problem was school transport. The country children had been caught up in a bomb scare and could not get home so once again the bishop passed the problem to the administrator and the administrator passed it on to the curate. In our parish, the curate was called Con and he knew everything if it was not too theological. If you wanted to convert your hall from a flat roof to a vaulted ceiling he was your man. If the gears of your transit van were not responding in a way that the Ford Motor Company would have expected it was Con who was called upon and who put things right again. So the transport problems of the country children were laid in Con's lap and he was told to get on with it. Other clerics might have washed their hands of the entire problem. Definitely, transport for children was not their responsibility.

Con, on the other hand, tackled the problem as he always did. No questions, no complaints, no requests for additional funds. He borrowed the minibus, or the van as it was called, from the youth club and at 3.00 p.m. every day he collected the country children and delivered every one of them to his or her doorstep and at 8.30 a.m. every morning he collected them from the same doorstep and delivered them safely to the school. And he continued to do this for the next ten years, day in, day out, with no exceptions, with no breaks, no reward, except what the children gave him, and no recognition from the powers that be. I don't think Con ever noticed that he was being used in the most outrageous fashion. His focus was as always getting the job done.

He was always a dedicated priest and that meant dedicated care and concern for his flock, but frequently they were ungrateful and unconcerned. Indeed there were those of a different political outlook who regarded him as 'the enemy', or if not 'the enemy' at least an unenthusiastic ally. They had their own agenda and they had no time for anyone not committed to their cause. On this occasion a riot had broken out on Bishop Street and a policeman had been separated from his colleagues and was now marooned in a semi-detached house with no immediate hope of rescue. It was only a matter of time before someone whipped up the crowd and accused him of attacking their mother or of shooting their child or some other outrageous crime but very little was needed to inflame the mob and converting them from passive spectators to murderous thugs.

Some of the locals recognised the danger and ran to summon Con to the rescue. He checked the facts 'What house was the policeman in? Who was in the house with him? Were there lamp posts or telephone poles in front of the door of the house? Were there many people in front of the house? Were they dangerous, or merely spectators?'

With a very sketchy picture of the situation he jumped into his van, his long-serving school minibus, and stormed up to Bishop Street and around the corner, blowing his horn and chivvying people to get out of the way. He drove his van up on the footpath so that it could be accessed from its sliding side door and from nowhere else. He slipped back the door, rushed into the house and grabbed the young policeman by the arm and dragged him into the van, all the while trying to convince him that he was not being abducted, that he had come to the rescue and that he should keep his head down and his arse covered until they had gone some distance away from the scene. Con revved up the van mercilessly and drove it off the footpath at high speed while the onlookers scattered out of his path. He drove the young policeman to the Strand Road Barracks, let him out at the front gate and went back to his bed and left the rest of them to get on with their rioting.

Many years later he attended a function in the Guildhall and got into conversation with some local policemen. He told them the story of the rescue of their colleague in Bishop Street and they immediately asked his name and parish because they had never known who had rescued their colleague and they felt bad that it had never been recognised. They wanted to present him with a medal in recognition of his bravery, but to Con it would have been an embarrassment. 'How could you accept a medal for just doing your job?'

He continued to ferry the children to school until some parent complained about the comfort and the quality of his transport, and then he realised that they now regarded him as a paid functionary of the educational system. His ten years of service were never given any official recognition. He was moved to another parish and some of his more perpendicular colleagues claimed to be embarrassed by what they considered his un-clerical and inappropriate activity. The rest of us could only bow our heads in admiration of someone who regarded heroic activity as the standard behaviour of a Catholic priest.

False Alarm

If the alarm goes off in your church in the middle of the night, and your church lies in the middle of the Bogside in Derry, and the event happens in the middle of what were politely called the Troubles, you do not go charging in like the Seventh Cavalry to investigate. You recruit a colleague and you both approach the church quietly and nervously, while keeping a careful lookout for anything unusual. Only when you have satisfied yourself that nothing sinister is happening do you venture to open the sacristy door. Only a complete fool will go for the church door. If there is one place an intruder can ambush you it is of course behind the main door.

Once inside the sacristy – which is also given careful scrutiny – you throw on all the lights in the church – inside and out. No way are you going to explore a darkened church. When the whole church is lit up like a Christmas tree, then, and only then, do you venture into the sanctuary to confront the intruder or to identify the spider or the malfunction that has set off the alarm.

In such situations we usually came prepared to meet the standard intruder. First in line was the intoxicated parishioner, who from his more sober days knew his way into the church, but in his present state had no idea how to get out of it, and after a few fruitless attempts to locate the exit had fallen asleep on the altar steps. Second was the opportunist burglar, who figured that since the priest used gold and silver vessels for offering Mass he might have a few other valuable trinkets somewhere about the premises, not to mention the possibility that the sacristan had locked away the Sunday collection in a cupboard with the intention of counting it at a later date. And third in line was the newly arrived terrorist or patriot or revolutionary – whichever way you wanted to view things – who was intent on stowing away some of the tools of his trade in a place where the constabulary would be least likely to find it; or to put it a little more bluntly, who was stashing guns and ammunition in my confession box, where he could retrieve them without interference on the occasion of the next military funeral.

On this occasion it was none of these three. It was a well-dressed lady – dark business suit and sensible shoes – who was standing before the altar, her face a ghastly white and an expression that would not have been out of place on a recently resurrected member of the undead. In her hand she clutched a pair of rosary beads.

It is perhaps indicative of the paranoia that we laboured under that while we figured she was an unlikely burglar we also considered that she might be some kind of stalking horse or agent provocateur. However, after a cursory examination we concluded that she did not really measure up to the specifications of a modern day Mata Hari. To the inexperienced eye, and both of us could claim to have less experience than most, it seemed that her face and her figure were more comfortable than would be considered necessary for even an amateur Mata Hari. We concluded, though on the basis of very flimsy concrete evidence, that she was not going to blow us up or shoot us in cold blood, so we approached her gingerly and invited her to join us in a cup of tea in the sacristy.

It was a new experience for both of us, but we instinctively avoided giving the impression of two rather bleary policemen about to interrogate a suspect and though, for the present, asking no details about personal identity or circumstances of life, we gently suggested that she might like to give us a reason for being in the church at this ungodly hour of night.

Slowly and gradually the story unfolded, and it was the stuff of nightmares. She had come to church for evening Mass, which started at half past seven, with the intention of going to Confession beforehand. Each evening the priest heard confessions for half an hour in the old Victorian-style confession box at the side of the church. It consisted of three compartments, each the dimensions of a free-standing wardrobe. The priest sat in the middle compartment the penitents knelt in the compartments on either side. Confession was heard through a small grill with a sliding door, and when the priest had finished with one penitent he closed the slide on that side and opened the slide on the other. This allowed a new penitent time to settle in and be prepared, while waiting for the priest to hear the confession on the other side. Of course the length of the wait depended on the other penitent. If he were long-winded, or had major issues to discuss with the priest, the delay could be prolonged, and this is what happened to our lady intruder. Because she had a serious personal issue she wished to discuss with the priest she had taken a small libation to give her some Dutch courage before coming to church. When she entered the confession box she was already a bit drowsy, and the other penitent was so long-winded that she eventually slid to the floor of the confession box, fast asleep. When the priest eventually pulled back his sliding door there was no one to be seen or heard, so he assumed that confessions had finished and went off to say Mass.

The lady slept through Mass, and continued sleeping while the congregation departed and the sacristan locked up the church for the night and set the alarm. At half past eleven the lady awoke. She was in pitch darkness, and initially she had no memory of where she was, and when she reached out to try to identify her surroundings she could touch nothing but timber walls – front and back of her, below her and above her. She must be in some kind of wooden container, it seemed. At that point panic set in. She had heard stories about people being buried alive and her life and her sins – especially her sins – flashed before her, and moved her to give her unexpurgated version of a God who would entice you into a confession box and then bury you alive before you had time to confess.

The thought drove her to desperate efforts. She pushed with all her might against the wooden walls one by one in a bid to escape until finally a door sprang open and she stumbled out into the church. The lock on the penitent's door was a ball and socket affair installed for that very purpose, so that no one would ever be locked in. All they had to do was push and they could escape.

She was obviously very upset by the incident and we comforted her as best we could and then took her home, but as we returned to base we could not help laughing incessantly because with the best will in the world no one could have prevented such an occurrence, for no one could have predicted or anticipated it. In fact, no one could have invented it, for truth is always so much stranger than fiction.

Confronting the Powerful

Last Friday I felt rather proud to be a priest of the Derry Diocese. It's a long time since I felt that way. I had just finished reading the account of Fr Joe Carolan's evidence to the Saville Inquiry. Sadly, it was historical evidence rather than personal.

Joe died very recently from cancer and was not there to give his account in person, and what an account it would have been!

No one would claim that Fr Joe was an intellectual giant or a subtle manipulator of the mass media. He was a simple and sincere Catholic priest who believed passionately that he had been called by God to give his life and his talents to the people of God in whatever way he was best able to serve them.

He wasn't always sure how this could be achieved, but he threw himself into his work with a passion and an innocence that merely served notice of the steely determination that he subsequently displayed in the defence of his flock. He was not going to do anything to besmirch or tarnish it. He was going to be – at the highest level – a priest forever, a priest like Melchizedek of old.

And then, set against this high and lofty ideal, against this attitude of sincerity and sacrifice, came the report in the same paper on Friday of a priest – yet another 'paedophile priest' – living only a few miles away from us, whose ghastly sins have finally caught up with him; whose depravity has undermined not just the faith but the basic humanity of countless victims; a sick, destructive force that has blighted the youth of so many innocent children and exposed them to elements of which they had no knowledge and forces against which they had no defence. It was so heartbreaking to read about both these men in the same newspaper, to believe for a moment that they had any affinity.

They came from the same generation. They responded to a call that was idealistic and noble, and yet was couched in terms that compelled even those with no enthusiasm for the rule to offer their lives for the redemption of the world and for the defeat of sin.

They responded to the call, not by asking 'How can I serve?' but by asking 'How can I not serve? Can I justify walking away from this high ideal that is set before me?' And many well-meaning but uncertain candidates for the priesthood plunged themselves into the clerical life hoping that somehow they would find a road that led to salvation.

Some did indeed reach a working arrangement with their priesthood, despite often feeling like square pegs in the proverbial round hole, but they persevered and made the best of it. Sadly, some never made it. The luckier ones abandoned their clerical role, sometimes under the guise of theological problems or devotional difficulties, and made no further claims on the priesthood.

The unluckier – or perhaps the sadder – stayed in the ranks and hoped to conceal their aridity by the constant shuffle of liturgical activity that passed for spiritual life. Some were merely gauche and sexually immature, and embarrassed themselves more than others by their pitiful fumblings; but lurking in the shadows were the predators, those mysteriously obsessed defilers who returned again and again to perpetrate the same obscenity on the victims least able to defend themselves. We didn't attack them and we didn't defend ourselves or our children from them. We were so innocent that we could completely understand and identify with the political leader who in the same predicament had to ask his closest adviser what a paedophile was, for we had no idea of what was involved. Sin we understood, and there were plenty of occasions for sin, but disease was outside our experience, and we let it spread and grow without hindrance.

It all seems so far removed from Fr Joe Carolan, stopped at a checkpoint on the bridge on Bloody Sunday, telling the soldier and the 'fat' policeman that they could start shooting because he was heading back into the fray whether they liked it or not. Joe was quite willing to confront the powers of the world in the pursuit of his duty. When sufficiently aroused he was quite willing to die in the fulfilment of his responsibilities as a Catholic priest, for he saw himself in terms of that proud tradition of service and sacrifice, which was the ideal of priesthood in which he had grown up, and he had no hesitation in offering his life if that was what the moment called for. Along with others like Fr Tony Mulvey and Fr Tom O'Gara, who are dead, and many others who are still alive, he was prepared to chance his life in the execution of his duty for that was how he had been taught and that was the commitment he made on the day of his ordination. He took his priesthood very seriously.

In the annals of history who will be remembered? The priest who had laid his life on the line and said, 'Shoot me if you have to, but I must be about my Father's business,' or the priest who added one more nail to the title plate 'paedophile priest'?

The awful reality of life is that one careless sinner can undo the lifetime work of ten dedicated saints. Forevermore the clergy of the Catholic Church will have to live with the myth that somehow they have a greater tendency to paedophilia than all others, that they have chosen this way of life in order to prey on the innocent and the vulnerable, that they used their power to protect the paedophile.

No amount of protesting about the privation or the discipline that candidates for the priesthood underwent during seven years of training will suffice to remove that suspicion. It will always infect people's attitudes and warp their motives so that the good will and the respect of decades will go unnoticed.

But now and then a flame from the past will flare up and illuminate for a moment the priest's world as it really was – the unlikely hero, the uncertain leader, the wounded healer, but always the resolute defender in time of danger of his own people. His actions did not follow decisions arrived at after rational analysis of the situation. They were as instinctive as a mother protecting her children.

On that night of Bloody Sunday, Fr Joe Carolan may have lain awake in his bed thinking of what had happened, terrified by his own audacity, but like the legendary chaplains of World War One, he was back on the street the next day, looking out over no man's land, waiting apprehensively for a new battle to commence. Posterity owes him, and others like him, a better epitaph than he has yet received.

Soldiers

I can remember as a child, standing by the roadside while a huge convoy of army tanks rumbled by before I could cross over. It was a common experience in those days. Sometimes it was tanks, sometimes five-tonne lorries with guns hitched behind, and sometimes just soldiers, either dressed in shorts and singlets and strung out along the road like exhausted marathon runners, or in full operations kit with heavy boots crashing on to the tarmac and singing, 'Roll me over in the clover, roll me over lay me down and do it again.' I heard that song so often in my childhood that I could sing it – verses and chorus – from start to finish. What I could not figure was why my mother got so hysterical when I tried to give a solo performance of it at home.

Soldiers, and the trappings of war, were a part of everyday life. If you woke in the morning and found a platoon of soldiers brewing up on the front lawn it was quite normal. You got dressed and went to school as usual. If you were warned to stay out of your fields because the army, next door, was practising with live mortar shells, it was quite normal. You merely waited until a Colonel Blimpish figure arrived on his white horse and took you around the fields while he counted the holes, for compensation purposes. It was equally normal to sneak back after he had gone and gather up the fins of the spent mortal shells – as long as you made sure they were spent. It was not normal when a schoolmate found a real one and took it home on the carrier of his bicycle and tried to dismantle it with a hammer. It was normal to peek over the training ground fence at some poor squaddie lying camouflaged in a bed of nettles and listen to his eloquent profanity as he urged you to get the hell off it before you betrayed his position.

It was all very normal, and very corrupting, for it taught us to regard war as a normal – and even a glamorous – way for the human race to settle its differences. We played at war, we talked about war, we made excuses for war. We breathed it in and out, like the air around us. War was the reality. Everything else was fantasy. Little wonder then that when the war ended and we eventually grew up we should be curious to know what happened to all our soldiers, with their lorries and their tanks and their guns. It seemed a harmless enquiry. After all, in the aftermath of every war one found books about the battles and the strategies and the commanders. But this was to be different. Our curiosity was so overpowering, our interest so morbid, that without knowing it we spawned a huge industry, creating a demand for a product that was in short supply, and as you know, where there is demand for a product there will always be someone to supply it.

War books became big business. Suddenly everyone with even a nodding acquaintance with the war was writing a book. The politician did it, and so too did the politician's doctor and the politician's bodyguard. The field marshal did it, and so too did the general, the colonel, the captain and even the private. The commodore, the commander, the sub-mariner, the codebreaker, the infiltrator, the prisoner, the escaper, the spy and the counterspy all added their nuggets of experience to the weightier collections of the historian and the war correspondent. And one amazing factor turned out to be common to all their books. They had all enjoyed the war. They may have been wet and hungry, pursued and shot at, imprisoned and tortured, but somehow the bad bits were erased, censored from their memories, and only the exciting and the uplifting bits remained to fill their books. They were all, it seemed, evangelists at heart. They brought only good news – or in cases of extreme necessity the bare bones of bad news.

Of course, it is not fair to blame the newcomers entirely for this alarming trend. They merely provided smaller, but more concentrated, doses of what the historians and the war correspondents had been dishing up for centuries. They reported the events of war, all right. They gave you the political ground-work and the battle plans and the numbers of dead and wounded, but they never gave you the appalling stink of battle, the gory savagery of men hacking one another to pieces and the sickening fear that turned hard men to jelly as the bombs and shells came bursting around them. If anything, you came away with the impression that war could be quite interesting, maybe even a welcome change from the dull routine of home and office. As a consequence the books increased and multiplied and soon the bookshops bulged with volumes dedicated to every aspect of war. They even had their own display units where war took its place alongside such immortal subjects as romance, classics, and do-it-yourself.

What is written about any war is unlikely to discourage people from going out to fight again and certainly not what was written about the Second World War. It was far too colourful and glamorous. Mind you, the later years of the First World War looked quite promising. So many young men had been killed, conditions in the trenches were appalling, and the prospect of victory so slim that there was a feeling of revulsion about war, a general disgust with it that eventually led to naming it 'The War to End All Wars'. However, it was not always so. The early years of the Great War were amazing. Some fool told the people that it would be over by Christmas, so young men volunteered in their thousands in the hope of a quick flash of glory and then safely home to mum and the girlfriend. The British writer Ian Hay wrote a book called *The First Hundred Thousand* about the early volunteers, which was very popular in its day, but which most of us would find hard to credit now. There is a marvellous sequence where everyone in the regiment is training enthusiastically except for one slacker – an Irishman, if my memory serves me – and he is hauled up in front of the Colonel. 'You do want to get to the front, O'Reilly,' says the Colonel. 'If your performance does not improve I am afraid I shall have no option but to leave you behind when the regiment does go into action.' Imagine a Vietnam conscript being given that kind of choice.

However, before the war was over some of these same volunteers were shooting holes in their feet or fomenting mutiny in order to get home. The glamour really faded out of the Great War, but the only one to remember the filth and the degradation was Eric Maria Remarque, author of *All Quiet on the Western Front* but he – the reader could console himself – was a German.

It took the rottenest of all wars – the Vietnam War – to raise the possibility, the suspicion – that perhaps war was not a good thing. It was only when the war had ended, and the soldiers had gone home and the politicians had stopped talking that the journalists and the helicopter pilots and the gunners could begin to tell their story. The neat news summaries and the optimistic editorials of the war years were discredited overnight. The mistakes, the atrocities, and the awful stench of war were vividly recalled. Likewise the overpowering fear of death, and the desperation to survive – a desperation that allowed no quarter and no compassion. The utter futility of the war – the inevitability of losing it – were freely admitted, for how can you defeat an enemy that you cannot see – friends and enemies look alike – and if you can see him how do you stop him if he is willing to climb over the bodies of his dead comrades in order to get at you. Other wars had occasional victories. This war was all defeats, for when you cleared a hill of the enemy today he was back in full possession of it a week later. And anyway, how did you kill an enemy who protected his guns with a shield of women and children – without killing them first – and if you did how did you live with the nightmares afterwards.

The troops saw the futility of it early on – and it drove some of them mad. The more obvious cases were invalided home and the less obvious ones looked at you like dead men, and booby trapped the officer's latrines with hand grenades. If they had won it might have seemed different, but they lost and lost badly. No one wanted to know them. For the first time ever, when Johnny came marching home the people turned out not to welcome him but to call him names. For all of them it was a bad war.

The professional soldier cannot be blamed for the horrors of war, but he makes it too easy for the politician. He enjoys the occasional war, so he fights without asking too many questions. A good war

– as he calls it – can mean rapid promotion, though it does not always work out according to plan. The American soldier who charged five German bunkers single handed on D-Day and killed over fifty of the enemy had a good war. The British Paratrooper, on the other hand, who answered a serious call of nature in the Falklands on the only ground available, the side of a steep rocky slope, and lost his balance and went skiing on his bare bottom right down the hill – for him it was a bad war, an indescribably bad war. He had to be invalided home – and how do you explain that kind of wound to your neighbours.

For us, every war is a bad war, because people die in it, and that is sinful, but perhaps the greatest blasphemy of war is that human beings devote so much virtue, so much courage, loyalty, endurance, and ingenuity to the sole purpose of killing other human beings.

Bloody Sunday

Back in 1972 I was a curate in a quiet country parish, reasonably insulated against the fires that were raging in many parts of the province. The Troubles – that strange title – in our locality had gone no further than someone setting fire to a Forestry Service truck, and someone else – or perhaps the same someone – attempting, for some arcane reason, to blow up the village sewage plant, giving rise to many scurrilous jokes about home industries and impaired output.

My hobby at that time was photography, and I had already made some amateurish attempts to chronicle the strange and frightening happenings that punctuated our lives, so when I learned that there was to be a major Civil Rights March in Derry on Sunday, 30 January I loaded my camera and set off, a veritable innocent abroad, to take a few photographs.

I should have been more aware of the risks, and of the danger. A short time previously I had been returning from a local talent competition with half a dozen of my protégés in the car, youngsters ranging from ten to sixteen years of age. We were in talkative mood for everyone had won some kind of prize, and though it was one o'clock in the morning the sudden appearance of a car closing up behind us and flashing its lights did not alarm us unduly. Maybe they were other revellers who had recognised the car, for we were less than a mile from home, but when we were forced to slow down by a particularly vicious bend in the road we heard the siren and we knew that we were being pursued by the forces of law and order and not by mischievous neighbours. We pulled up immediately and so did the other car, and two RUC officers and two military policemen jumped out with guns at the ready and ordered us out with our hands up.

They detained us for three hours by the roadside, or rather myself and the other adult were kept by the roadside, while the children were kept in the back seat and interrogated by the two military policemen. Neither Driving Licence nor Insurance Certificate was considered sufficient to establish my identity. The RUC officers insisted that their superiors had informed them by radio that no one answering my name or description lived in that area, and that I was consequently now under arrest and should accompany them forthwith. I said I had collected these children from their homes and I fully intended returning them to their homes before going anywhere.

By this time the soldiers had finished questioning the children and had concluded that we were not dangerous terrorists, so we were able to convince the policemen to follow us to my home where I presented them with further proofs of my identity, from photos on the wall to today's mail still lying in the hallway. Eventually, they accepted my word and departed, but at no time did anyone suggest that this was not an acceptable form of policing. These were dangerous times, for no one knew who was harmless and who was dangerous, so everyone was treated as dangerous, until proven otherwise. In the country areas we had little experience at the time of those dangers and consequently we tended to take foolish risks.

When I reached Derry on that memorable Sunday I wandered around the city walls overlooking the Bogside and attracted some curious and some unfriendly looks from the soldiers patrolling the walls or manning the various strong points, but clerical garb still provided a certain immunity in those days, so I wandered in and out through them and eventually came to a barricade at the mouth of William Street, and there I stood for the next hour and a half.

Nothing happened. I waited for the march to pass, pointing my camera over the shoulders of the soldiers, ready for one of those increasingly familiar action shots of a youthful rioter lobbing a stone or a petrol bomb at the forces of law and order. I waited, as I say, for an hour and a half and nothing happened. It was a bitterly cold day and the chill was beginning to get through to my skin as

I stood there. So I said, 'Forget it. There'll be other marches.' And I went home.

The first reports came through on the car radio as I neared home. Seven dead, they said, at that point, and the tally finally rose to thirteen. I could only think, 'God must really care for the feeble minded.' Only a half wit like myself could have positioned himself so disastrously that God had to step in and protect him with the weather. I had been the classic victim – in-waiting, in the wrong place at the wrong time, for if the stones hadn't got me the bullets would have. What I couldn't understand was why he had protected me and not the others. They had, after all, been trying in their own way to put right a wrong, whereas I was merely trying to record it.

It was all commemorated yesterday with marches and placards and speeches and all the paraphernalia of politics. For the families and friends of the victims, they can only commemorate it as the day on which innocence died. For me, I can only commemorate it as the day when providence once more stepped in and lifted me from the dangers surrounding me and set me down in the serenity of my country parish, safe from the horrors of the world around me, for at least another day.

Looking Down Upon Lough Foyle

It all looks so peaceful today but fifty years ago this entire valley was a hive of military activity. The City of Derry Airport down there was once the Eglinton Military Airfield, with army transit camps all around it; over there is Ballykelly, still a military airfield; and from these buildings behind me a communications network stretched across Europe in one direction and across the Atlantic in the other; and down there is the Port of Derry at Lisahally, where the German U-Board Fleet surrendered at the end of the war.

It was a fitting spot for the surrender, for it was from here that the escort ships set off into the Atlantic to guard the vital convoys from America, bringing in everything from oil to oatmeal, and where so many of them fell victim to the U-Boats. The early years of the war were little short of disastrous, and by 1943 the Allies were losing half a million tonnes of shipping every month. On other fronts there were no victories, but in the Atlantic there was a distinct possibility of defeat. The Germans had broken the British naval codes and the U-Boats were able to lie in ambush for the convoys, especially for the precious oil tankers.

By 1943, in fact, the news was so bad that it could not be told. A drawing of a drowning sailor covered in oil and clinging to a piece of wreckage appeared in a daily newspaper above the caption 'The price of petrol has just gone up by one penny'. It caused uproar because it undermined morale and was never printed again. Calamities such as the Canadian attack on Dieppe, where a mere 1,250 out of 5,000 returned home had to be dressed up as useful experience for the forthcoming invasion of Europe. The death of

600 American soldiers during a training exercise off Slapton sands, when German torpedo boats slipped in among the transports, was ruthlessly covered up and the survivors threatened with dire penalties if they breathed so much as a word about it. On 23 July 1944 the American Airforce dropped 700 tonnes of bombs on its own men, and repeated the performance on an even bigger scale the following day, killing, among many others, Lieutenant General Leslie McNair, the highest ranking Allied officer to die in North West Europe.

Who knows how many other disasters occurred which will never be reported? The war was a harsh and bitter experience for millions of innocent people, and a harsh and bitter death for the fifty million others who perished in it. It was all started by a man who believed that he was better than other men, and because he was better others must be worse, and if they were worse they were not important. The respect which every human being owes to every other human being was discarded, and very soon his followers were massacring men, women and children without a qualm.

The world has not changed and evil has not disappeared. Every time we distinguish between 'us' and 'them', every time we point a finger and say 'they are different', every time we belittle or sneer at someone's background or culture, every time we justify revenge and retaliation, every time we glorify violence, we are setting the world one step further along a course that will change this green and pleasant valley once again into a field of battle, too awful to describe.

Death in the Afternoon

I was visiting Bridget in her little terraced house in what the media mistakenly called the Bogside, and the world around us had ceased to exist. She was reminiscing about her young days, and she talked about her marriage and the joy of having her own place after so many years of hardship and congestion, and the awful trauma and pain when her husband took a heart attack and left her a widow with four children at twenty-nine years of age. But in the spirit of her time she had coped.

She had a profound compassion for everyone. She appreciated that people were still coping with hard times, and some were better at it than others, but they all struggled on and did the best they could amid the violence and the turmoil that surrounded them.

Essentially, Bridget was waiting to die, but she was not depressed or saddened by the prospect. She had a profound faith. In fact she was on first-name terms with God, and spoke to him freely and honestly. The only thing she missed was the neighbourliness of the past, and all the good people she had known, but otherwise she was ready to go.

We sat together in silence, looking out the window at the traffic, sharing the peace and quiet, when suddenly a car appeared at the top of the hill opposite us, travelling at a murderous speed, full headlights blazing, hazard lights flashing, and the horn beating out a tattoo that warned everyone to stay clear. This was clearly a major emergency but it gave no indication of who or what was involved. As the car slowed down to take the corner into the road in front of us, I was shocked to recognise the driver as my own curate. His eyes were firmly on the road, and he roared past us, entirely concentrated on getting somewhere as fast as possible. I raced to my own car, shouting to Bridget that I would call with her when I got a moment, and rushed to the Parochial House to find out what had happened.

No one was sure of the details but the essentials were undisputed. Several people were dead following a gunfight a few streets away. It took some time for all the facts to emerge, for the propaganda battle was always being fought and no one wanted to look bad.

British Military Intelligence in Northern Ireland frequently misread the culture of the working class areas when they tried to infiltrate Republican organisations. They tended to think of places such as Belfast or Derry the way cities like London or Manchester were cities, whereas there are no cities in Northern Ireland, merely large towns, where every newcomer to a district is identified not merely by a name but also by his relatives, his connections. If he tells us that his name is James McCloskey we want to know which McCloskey tribe he belongs to. Has he a nickname, who was his father, had they any connection with this place in the past, where had he lived previously, what kind of work did he do? Even his speech would be analysed. Did he use the idioms and terminology of the locality, greeting you with 'yes' in Derry or handing you your 'wee' receipt, or did he speak in a more neutral fashion? In a matter of days any inconsistency would be exposed – with possibly lethal consequences. This incident could have been the result of such carelessness. On the other hand, it could have been the result of a sinister double bluff.

A young military intelligence officer was sent into the Creggan area of Derry to learn anything he could about local Republican activity. He dressed in jeans and t-shirt and drove a rusty clapped-out car and tried to blend into the background as best he could, but he was most likely spotted for what he was before he had completed his second circuit of the estate.

Next time around four young men of Republican background were waiting in their own car, and they set off in pursuit, confident that with their local knowledge and their superiority in numbers they could easily ambush him. They followed him on to the main road bordering the estate, but instead of fleeing from his pursuers the young soldier stopped his car and stepped out. His pursuers did the same. They obviously intended closing in on their quarry with guns drawn. What they did not know, or see, was that their quarry was much better armed than any of them. He had a machine pistol, an Uzzi, much favoured by Israeli special forces, and he opened fire on his pursuers before they realised what was happening. In one burst he killed two of his pursuers and injured a third, and then stepped calmly into his transport and drove to his army base where, it is reported, he was greeted as a hero. Whether it was a coat-trailing exercise, or whether he was genuinely running for his life, no one knows, but locally, it was a bad day indeed.

In due course I returned to Bridget and gave her a brief account of the incident.

'My two sons are both left home now,' she said, 'but I worry have they been caught up in any of this. I sometimes worry have they even killed someone, for there are people out there who can persuade them that this is a right and patriotic thing to do.'

I tried to persuade her that her sons were all far removed from all this local madness, but she was not convinced. She watched the television, she watched the news, and she knew that young men were an easy target for the recruiting sergeants, and who knows, her children might have become victims.

The tears welled up in her eyes at the thought, and she automatically reached for her rosary beads. 'I'm afraid now, even in my own home. For the first time ever I'm afraid, because people are killing other people a street away from me. I don't feel safe anymore.'

She burst into tears and said, 'I wish it was all over.'

'We all wish it was over,' I replied, but I knew in my heart that was not what she meant.

Normal Violence

In the days of my childhood, many years ago, I firmly believed that I belonged to a very normal family. It had all the appearances of a normal family and it never occurred to me, or to any of my brothers or sisters, to question the accuracy of our perceptions. We were a normal family of three boys and five girls.

My father was a cattle dealer. He left home every day in the early hours of the morning to attend some cattle fair or other, but everyone was expected to speed his departure by helping with the milking of cows, the feeding of pigs, and various other farmyard chores that needed doing. It was normal, in our estimation, that everyone should work and expect no pay for it. Pocket money was a mere fantasy. It was also normal that we should get down on our knees to pray as soon as we rose from our beds. It was normal to recite the rosary every night, even if the mind tended to wander to other things. It was normal to go to Confession every Saturday night and to eight o'clock Mass every Sunday morning and sit as a family in the same pew. It was normal to attend school every day without exception and to face the violence of fellow pupils and teachers without complaint. It was normal, as Sam McAughtry put it, to study Shakespeare at the end of a fist. Indeed, even religion was studied at the end of some equally blunt instrument. Away from school, it was normal to encounter vast arrays of tanks and guns and soldiers in uniform, and in your home it was normal to pick up a newspaper and read that this man or that women had been executed by hanging at nine o'clock that morning.

Violence, fear and intimidation lay at the heart of our culture. Work, duty, discipline and unquestioning obedience were the basics of our civic and religious life. We responded promptly to the commands of parents, teachers, clergy, policemen, or any other figures of authority and lived with the fear of punishment, for only by the sharp application of physical punishment was it believed that we would overcome our tendency to squander our time and our talents. In short, we acknowledged the hand of authority in whatever quarter it was raised and never thought of defying it.

Small wonder then that when faced with Christ's injunction to Peter to 'feed my lambs, feed my sheep' we tended to ask, 'Who owns these sheep?' 'Who has the right to feed these sheep?' We were more concerned about authority and control than about pastoral care. If these were Peter's sheep, then he alone had the right to feed them. We didn't focus on the fact that they might be sick or straying on the mountainside or confused. We were in full agreement with a Peter who said, 'You now belong to my flock. These are the rules in my flock and I expect them to be obeyed. And if you don't like these rules you can leave. We want no doubters or questioners here.'

It took us a long time to even question our normality, but eventually we grew to an awareness that our God was not a God of vengeance and violence and retribution but a God of compassion and understanding and forgiveness. We began to see that love and respect brought us far closer to God than all our righteous observance of rules and regulations. We eventually realised that fear was not the basis of a proper relationship between pupil and teacher, much less between child and parent. We saw that war was an insanely destructive way of settling differences. We learned that capital punishment deterred no one but merely devalued the precious gift of human life. In short, we found a new and more sympathetic way of looking at people, especially people who had sinned. We still heard the voice of Christ saying, 'Feed my lambs, feed my sheep,' but we saw leadership in a completely new light. It was no longer the mere exercise of authority. It was a delicate relationship between those who were chosen and those who chose to follow, and if the followers did not follow, the leaders were powerless. Sadly, we were slow to learn the lesson.

While experts in the business world were holding management seminars and highlighting the importance of consultation, we were still defending our right to lay down the law. But we made progress in spite of ourselves. Like Peter, we found ourselves being led along ways where we would rather not go, but the discovery of our failings helped us to be more compassionate towards others.

However, the process was time-consuming and the results were often ragged and untidy. There were no instant solutions, and some people began to look back with nostalgia at the good old days. 'There was respect for the law back then. If you stepped out of line you got punished. People could walk the streets in safety' and so on. It may not have been Fascism but it marched to the same tune. 'Bring back the death penalty. Longer jail sentences. Make them pay for their crimes.'

The real danger was, and still is, that the discontent will spread to the Church, that someone will believe that a return to the old severities will restore the old security and the old certainty.

It won't work. It never has worked, for there are no clean-cut solutions to human problems. People will always be tempted to be selfish and short-sighted and unreasonable, and only patient compassion and love will cause them to change. Leadership will always be a learning process where yesterday's mistakes will shape the lessons of tomorrow. We cannot be stern judges of our peoples' failings. We have to follow in the steps of Christ who went in search of the lost sheep, who would not break the crushed reed nor quench the wavering flame, who proclaimed 'I have come not to call the just but sinners to repentance', who felt sorry for the crowd because they were harassed and dejected like sheep without a shepherd, who cried out to everyone: 'Come to me all you who labour and are overburdened and I will give you rest.'

Rudolph's Christmas

I can tell you straight off I'm not looking forward to this trip to Derry, not after last year's fiasco. I mean, a reindeer's life is tough enough at the best of times. We may have a bit of glamour and publicity at Christmas, but for the rest of the year we have to put up with endless snow and the awful boredom of hanging around, doing nothing. Then suddenly in the last month of the year the whole place goes completely berserk.

There's Santa and Robert the Elf and the Christmas Fairy and all the rest of the staff ploughing through mountains of letters trying to get them into some kind of order for the delivery department. It doesn't help Santa's temper anything either, for he has to vet all those letters personally to see who's going to get what, but as soon as he has a batch of them sorted he sends them over to the warehouse, and that's where we come in. We have to pull these huge sleighs around the counters while they're being filled with presents and every year the toys seem to get bigger and heavier. A generation ago it was all little dolls and stuffed animals, but now its BMX bicycles, electronic organs, computers, typewriters, games sets, you name it; if its big and heavy you can be sure its on the list.

In fact, things got so bad last year we formed a trade union and I was elected to present Santa with a list of our demands. I thought they were all very reasonable – like a limit on the load a sleigh would carry, free issue of leg warmers for all reindeers, extra hay for working unsociable hours, and I also included a little personal note that calling me Red Nose would stop immediately.

On reflection, now, I suppose it wasn't a good time to threaten a strike. You know what employers think of trade unions these days, but even so I wasn't prepared for the lambasting that Santa gave us. 'Listen, Brothers,' he said, very sarcastic like, 'It may have escaped your notice that we're in the middle of a recession, not to mention the fact that this is very seasonal work we do. It's so seasonal, in fact, it's almost gone before you know it has arrived, so there's no room for freeloading and feather-bedding in this firm. Either you get stuck into it and make your deliveries on time as usual, or you can collect your cards right now from the office. There are plenty of unemployed reindeers who'd be only too happy to work. And in case Mr Rudolph you're getting any elevated notions about your importance to this whole project because somebody wrote a song about you, just remember that it was pure accident you caught a head cold that year and brought your inflamed hooter to everybody's attention. But ever since it has been my little brush and a tin of fluorescent paint that has kept you in the limelight. And, to me, one reindeer's nose is as easy to paint as another, so unless you want to be the best known unemployed reindeer in Santa Land, get into your harness and start pulling.'

That was the end of that strike, I can tell you. But to get back to last year's trip. Everything went off quite smoothly at first. We got the sleigh loaded and set off as usual. Santa left most of the navigation to me. At the time I had no idea of the danger. I always try to keep out of the regular airline routes, not because there was any risk of a crash but we had heard we were getting all the children in the airplanes into trouble. You see grown ups can only see us if we're very close to them, so just for the fun of it we used to trot alongside these big jumbo jets at 30,000 feet and Santa would wave at any children on board and of course they waved back and shouted to their mammys that they could see Santa Claus. But of course the grown ups couldn't see a thing and between one thing and another it sometimes finished up with our best customers getting a painful smack from mammy for telling lies.

So last year I decided to pick a nice quiet route where there would be very little air traffic. And where better than over Russia.

They never seem to have too many planes flying in their airspace. But I figured something was wrong when two MiG Fighters came storming up behind us and the pilots started jabbering to one another on the radio. Fortunately they were adults and couldn't see us, though obviously their ground radar had told them there was something up there.

Anyway, I got out of there as fast as I could and set course for Derry. And we eventually came in for a nice gentle landing down at Culmore. Santa said we would start down there because there was a nice class of people with new houses and big chimneys. However, he obviously forgot that they were touchy about their new roofs because we had hardly started work when a nice little boy in a blue dressing gown and slippers, came out and said his daddy wanted to know who was thumping around on his roof. So of course, Santa introduced himself and the young man duly conveyed the message indoors to daddy, but in no time at all he was out again. This time to inform us that his daddy didn't care it was Superman, to get those reindeers down off his roof, and a whole lot more about the cost of tiles and the difficulty of replacing broken ones and so on. So to keep the peace, Santa ordered us to park the sleigh in the roadway. It wasn't very convenient but we managed and at one point we even got fed by some of the locals. Pâté sandwiches and Babycham, would you believe? But I suppose it's the thought that counts.

Then on up to the Bogside and again we started having problems. I was down in the street and I could hear Santa rattling and thumping around on the roofs, and it eventually got so noisy that I called up to ask him what was the matter. 'I can't find the chimney,' he replied. You'd think he would keep his records up to date. I told him they had given up building chimneys in the Bogside years ago, and to try a window or slide down the television aerial. I know he hates coming down TV aerials because he's so fat he has to suck in his stomach and hold his breath the whole way down. Anyway, he eventually got started, but they've been moving house so much recently in the Bogside that he got mixed up and landed in a house where there was no one but a little old lady. I could see him through the window desperately trying to be polite and at the same time looking at his watch and edging towards the door. But she had him well and truly trapped. She chatted to him as if she had known him all her life and fairly smothered him with good will and gossip. 'Sit down son and rest yourself until I get you a cup of tea. You must be worn out. You need to mind yourself at your time of day, you could get one of them coronary thromboses and it would take ye off in a flash. And look at them poor wee donkeys out there pulling that cart, and them up to their oxters in snow.' And out the door she came and put a long woollen scarf around my neck and said, 'There ye are Neddy. Wrap that round ye and keep your chest warm.' And then back into the house and on again without catching her breath, 'And you ought to put a sensible hat on them wee animals to keep their ears warm instead of them oul' withered branches' and on and on she went. I was so fascinated by the whole business and by Santa's futile efforts to explain that he had landed in the wrong house that when I eventually looked around me again I could hardly believe my eyes, for here was this little gang of nippers coming up the street towards me. I mean, Christmas night and they're not even in their beds. 'Yes, Rudolph,' says one to me, and the other says 'How's about ye!' And third squeezes my nose and goes 'Honk, honk, honk.' Now if there's one thing that really annoys me its people squeezing my noise and going 'Honk, honk, honk.' I was seriously contemplating retaliation, despite all of Santa's rules, but before I knew what was happening one of them pulled out an aerosol can and sprayed 'UTP' in big letters across Blitzen's rump, while another tried to unscrew Donner's antlers. I just yelled for Santa and he came running out all red-faced and sweaty, but because they were children he starting doing his 'Ho, Ho, Ho' and 'Well my little man' act. It was obviously the wrong approach. They just calmly looked him in the eye and said, 'On yer bike, Fatso.' We figured it was time to leave.

All of this did nothing to improve Santa's temper, so when we were crossing the bridge and ran into a police checkpoint I knew there was going to be trouble. A big policeman waved us down with his red lamp and after looking at Santa for a long time said, 'Have you any means of identification, Sir?' I mean, it's not the kind of question Santa is usually asked. So he got a big aggressive and said 'Who do you think I am? The Lord Mayor?' It was the wrong answer. 'Step out of the vehicle, Sir, and put your hands on the bonnet,' said the policeman and the tone of his voice told Santa not to argue. So out he got, and they patted him up and down, and looked under his hat, and then more questions. 'Are you the owner of this vehicle, Sir? Are you aware you need a PSV licence for a goods vehicle Sir? Incidentally Sir, what kind of goods are you transporting?' The very suggestion that there might be something dodgy about his cargo made Santa so indignant that he jumped on the sleigh and grabbed for the nearest parcel to prove his innocence, but in the process lost his footing and fell head first into the middle of the load. 'Have you been drinking, Sir?' said the policeman, and without waiting for an answer produced a little plastic bag and said, 'I'd like you to blow into this, Sir.' Fortunately just then one of the younger policemen obviously remembered who Santa was and whispered into his colleague's ear, 'He's Santa Claus. You remember him, he comes at Christmas. Santa Claus started out as St Nicholas.' 'Oh, he's a clergyman,' said the big policeman, on familiar ground at last, and immediately switched his stance for he was well used to dealing with awkward clergymen. 'That will be alright, Reverend, just continue on your way.' And off we went once more.

The rest of the night followed much the same pattern. In one area a couple of comedians painted the tailgate of the sleigh blue, and in another, a couple of figures in balaclava helmets tried to hijack us. I was mightily relieved, I can tell you, when we eventually got clear of the city, and Santa stopped for a little breather at a little church away up on the hills above Muff. It was a peaceful little place, for the only sound seemed to come from far away. There was a little crib in the corner and Santa sat down in front of it and for a long time he just sat and looked at the figures of Mary and Joseph and the baby Jesus. When he eventually got up to go, he looked back over his shoulder at the figure of the baby and said 'Son, you really have your work cut out.'

Lent

No account of Catholic Lenten practice is complete without the story of the British Army's first introduction to a traditional Irish Ash Wednesday. The script is derived from a two-way radio conversation between a little soldier on the top of the Embassy Building in Derry, looking down over what he mistakenly calls the Bogside, and his headquarters in some other part of the city. I will not even attempt the accents.

'Alpha Romeo, Alpha Romeo to base.'

'Base here, Alpha Romeo. What is it?'

'Base, there is something strange going on here.'

'Alpha Romeo, what do you mean strange?'

'Base, there's a large crowd of people coming out of a church and they all have some kind of mark on their foreheads.'

'Alpha Romeo, what colour is this mark?'

'It's black, Base; right in the middle of their foreheads.'

'Alpha Romeo, are they all men, these people?'

'No, Base. There's women and children, and they have black marks on their foreheads as well.'

'Alpha Romeo, can you see are any of these people carrying weapons?'

'Weapons, Base? Some of the women are carrying shopping bags.'

'Alpha Romeo, stand by; I'll have to seek guidance on this one.'

A long pause follows, and then, 'Alpha Romeo, it's alright. You can relax. Apparently this is something which the priests do to them every year about this time.'

And so another clash of contrasting cultures is resolved.

Ashes on the forehead mark the beginning of Lent for us Catholics. We make a public declaration of allegiance – whether we like it or not. Some adults are a bit self-conscious in these fragile times, but children flaunt their ashes like banners, and compete with one another for the biggest spread and the best pattern. They take Lent very seriously and they figure it is only right and proper that the Church should set its seal on them in a manner worthy of the occasion.

Your own experience may be different, but in my young days you started Lent by acquiring a Parrish's Chemical Food dried-milk tin. This was done by visiting any of the neighbours with a baby in the house before Lent and putting in your requisition. This was to be your sweety tin for Lent. You would no longer eat sweets; instead, you would squirrel them all away in this tin for the duration. However, mothers took advantage of Lent to economise. When they went shopping the customary bag of sweets was now omitted. This was Lent, you were reminded. Christ fasted for forty days; the least you could do is give up sweets.

So we learned to live with adversity, and sometimes took advantage of it. We visited neighbours with our tin in our hands and timidly suggested that if they had any spare sweets lying around the house they might like to contribute. Visitors were screened for goodies and if they didn't cough up the first time they were gently reminded that it was an acceptable social practice to bring a few donations for the child's sweety tin the next time around.

In a large family this could create unhealthy competition. A friend told me that her sister hid her sweety tin in a hawthorn hedge but her brother discovered it, and by the laws of buried treasure or whatever, he felt entitled to transfer a couple of sweets from her tin to his own. When the sister found out she yelled for retribution and brought it to the attention of her father, a man of few but very incisive words. In a gesture reminiscent of the prophet Daniel he took both tins and hurled the contents into the fire with a crisp 'and now everybody has the same amount'. The same lady told me that in her house during Lent no raisins were put into the soda bread – even caraway seeds were forbidden –

and the two pound pot of jam was locked away for the duration of Lent. Teenagers, of course had a different agenda. They gave up dances and the cinema for Lent and grown-ups gave up grown-up vices like smoking and drinking.

A surprising number of them lasted the pace, and still do for that matter, for the pattern of Lenten sacrifice has changed very little over the years. It is not that we think we will become men and women of iron will if we deny ourselves luxuries, or that we will somehow atone for the sins of the world, but there is a feeling of solidarity with Christ. We figure that if he is fasting in the heat of the desert for forty days we shouldn't be sitting down alongside him with a pint of cold beer in one hand a chicken sandwich in the other.

The Bits In Between

Employment

Since finding myself cast in the unlikely – and unwanted – role of employer I think I have finally cracked the problem of the present economic recession.

It has nothing to do with economic policy, or the pressure of inflation. It is just that the entire body of bureaucrats – the civil service, the banks, the insurance companies and the accounting professions – have created a jungle of paperwork through which no one can travel in safety without their guidance, and brazenly add to it every year so only those who can afford the services of these experts before they begin can hope to survive the journey – thus effectively sabotaging anyone who tries to begin at the bottom and work his way up. Far from encouraging employment, successive governments have made it inevitable that no one will even attempt to create new jobs.

I think this whole thing can be easiest explained if I relate it in the form of a cautionary tale entitled 'The decline and fall of Joe Bloggs' or 'You can't beat the bureaucrats'.

Joe Bloggs was a typical young man of his times – no formal academic qualifications but a course in foundation studies at Magee University – and he had never worked a day in his life. He occasionally helped out his grandmother in her little corner shop, and when she died he was pleasantly surprised to learn that she had left him the business – lock, stock and barrel. He was a bit hesitant about taking it on – even such a minor business – without training or experience, but he felt he owed it to his grandmother to give it a try; so come Monday morning Joe rolled back the shutters and opened for business.

It was all much easier than he had expected. He sold what was on the shelves, and as the stocks dwindled a very helpful young man from the wholesalers – full of pleasantries and encouragement – called around and took orders for whatever he needed.

His father warned him about insurance – in case the shop burned down some night – so he nipped down to the insurance broker and asked him for insurance against fire and other likely hazards. It surprised him somewhat to discover that the other hazards included theft, hold-ups, cash, glass, engineering, employer's liability, public liability, all risks, consequential loss, and personal accident, all of them requiring insurance cover. Nonetheless Joe persevered, and bit by bit he began to get the business off the ground, because he worked long hours and was always pleasant to the customers, even when he knew that they were dealing with him only because they had forgotten a particular item at the supermarket.

One thing, however, shocked him. When he brought his takings to the bank, having carefully sorted and counted them, he was charged a fee for every penny he lodged – 44p for every £100 – and another fee for every cheque he wrote. They didn't seem to welcome his money. It puzzled Joe that he had not heard of this practice before, but when he investigated he discovered that it was restricted to business accounts, such as himself, and had no effect whatever on those who didn't try to start businesses. Joe also discovered, the hard way, that he was now expected to pay £4.50 per week – National Insurance contributions, it was called – for the privilege of being self-employed. He even got used to the little men who came to inspect his scales, or to talk to him, as they put it, 'about matters relating to value added tax'. At this stage of his career Joe had never even heard of the dreaded 'VAT Man' but he was soon to learn that, next to God, there was no one with such far-reaching and unlimited powers.

Nonetheless, Joe struggled on.

The long hours were beginning to take their toll so he decided to employ some help – and hired a rather brassy young lady called Jacqueline. She was supposed to bring a document called a P45 with her, but Jacqueline merely shrugged her shoulders and said she'd never heard of it. Joe contacted the tax office and was told that if he collected forms P15 and P46 and filled them in they would issue Jacqueline with a P45. In the meantime he should simply put her on an emergency code. Needless to say, this led to some further enquiries and Joe was astonished to find that the tax office not merely expected him to pay Jacqueline's wages, but that he had to collect Jacqueline's income tax each week, keep exact records of it (on a P11) and pay it in to the tax office every month. And that was only the beginning. He was also responsible for collecting and paying her National Insurance contributions, as well as a large extra slice of National Insurance for himself. In case he had any difficulty with all this they gave him a sheaf of P11s, a blue P8 to explain the P11, an employer's guide to PAYE (all sixty-seven pages of it), an employer's guide to National Insurance contributions (forty-six pages) and an employer's guide to Statutory Sick Pay (fifty-nine pages). In addition he was given three large books of tables, one for calculating taxable pay, one for free pay, and one for Not-contracted-out National Insurance contributions and Statutory Sick Pay.

Joe took them all home with him and studied them far into the night, but he couldn't make head or tail of them. Even the explanations were more complicated than the problems. He kept running across things like:

> certificates of reduced liability on form CF 380 or tear off notice (form CF 2 AR (TO)) etc. from a 1974/75 National Insurance Card should have been exchanged for certificates of election (form CF 383) and should not be accepted as evidence of reduced liability after that date.

Even the P11, which was supposed to be the easy one, had him flummoxed. It was supposed to provide a yearly record of all payments of wages, tax, and National Insurance, week by week, but it was full of strange anomalies. The year, for instance, did not start on 1 January, like every other year Joe knew about, but on 6 April, and every year did not have fifty-two weeks as he had been taught at school. Some had fifty-three, and likewise some months had five weeks instead of four. And if you were paid on a Thursday and the sixth fell on a Friday there was a possibility that the year would begin on the twelfth. To add to the confusion there were all these columns about total pay and taxable pay and free pay and National Insurance contributions at contracted out rate.

Joe went to bed with a sore head, and next day the post brought him more forms – a P35, a stack of SSP2s and a note that they would send him a P6 if there was any change in his employee's coding. That night he tackled them manfully again and persevered for many more nights thereafter, but the long working days and sleepless nights were beginning to play havoc with his health. He struggled on with his shopkeeping and tried to cope with the sanitary inspector who insisted on new toilets, the architect who drew up the plans, the planning authorities who sent them back for revision, the contractor who was late in starting and the man from building control who inspected everything, but the descent into hell had already begun, and Jacqueline helped to speed it up. She wasn't a bad soul, but she knew nothing about shopkeeping. If Joe mentioned punctuality, or her unfortunate tendency to gossip about one customer to another, she went into a huff and refused to speak to anyone, employer or customers, for the rest of the day, with the result that some unreasonable customers regarded her anger as directed at them and never came back again. Joe decided that the time had come for him to take steps. Enough was enough. He would sack her before she wrecked the business completely, so in a moment of desperation he took his courage in his hands and asked her to go. She went – but not for long. A week later the post brought him a summons to appear before a tribunal and justify his use of the word 'inefficient' on her X15. It was defamation of character, her legal-aid lawyer claimed. Once again Joe had to pay for professional help and despite his lawyer's efforts the man in charge found in favour of Jacqueline, said youthful indiscretion was hardly grounds for dismissal and expressed surprise that a man in Joe's position did not have a better acquaintance with the Industrial Relations Act.

The thought of another book of rules that he hadn't even heard about finally cracked Joe. His health gave up completely. His parents closed down the shop and Joe spent his time wandering aimlessly about the house compulsively filling in every blank form he could find, and having nightmares about little men trying to stone him to death with handfuls of P11s. The end came when, finally and reluctantly, his parents signed him into a psychiatric hospital, and as the men in white coats led him away he could be heard shouting, 'You can't do this to me. You haven't filled in a P45.'

Finding God in a Morris Eight

In my student days they used to warn us in the logic class about a nasty affliction called the 'syllogistic jump'. It is the kind of thing that happens when you make an assumption that is not justified. For example, a car passes you on the road. You assume there is a driver in it but in fact it may be a runaway. The same mistake occurs when it is assumed that someone wearing clerical garb will have an earlier and a deeper experience of God than anyone else whereas the truth is that the relentless routine of services, sacraments and sacred office can often be the biggest obstacle that clergy encounter on their way to God. If a gentle breeze is supposed to enfold the presence of the Almighty there is little chance of finding him in the neurotic paranoia of parish life.

All that, however, is another way of saying that I have very little experience of God, but I do have a reasonable degree of awareness. 'Experiences' in my childhood were confined to such events as getting lost, or a sudden skelp from a dishcloth, or having a nightmare. God, on the other hand, was supposed to be impartial and merciful so your relationship with Him was more of a gentle awareness than a memorable experience.

Certain people, places and things reminded you of God, and for me the most important of these reminders was a 1936 two-door Morris Eight saloon. It was the kind of car that antique car fanatics now refurbish – and even rebuild – and transport on custom-built trailers to rallies where they bask in the vicarious admiration of the crowd. In those days it was strictly a means of transport – for shifting all ten of us, parents and eight children, to church every

Saturday night and Sunday morning. (In case you are wondering how you got ten people into a Morris Eight, it is done exactly like the elephant joke – two in the front and eight in the back. As for the Saturday night and Sunday morning, in those days Saturday night Confession was almost as sacrosanct as Sunday morning Mass.)

Now, had it been an ordinary car that started when you turned the key, it would have been forgotten years ago. Instead, it was a cantankerous death-trap of dubious origins and unpredictable behaviour. It never started if you were in a hurry, and no amount of mechanical torque applied to the starting handle or direct energy applied to pushing made any difference. It started when it wanted to – and that could be with the first turn of the key, or half an hour later when it had already been pushed a large part of the journey under protest.

Once under way, however, we piled in and the obligatory prayers were started, and these continued until we reached the church. They were mostly what used to be called 'aspirations', short little sentences of praise or thanksgiving or petition which swooped about in a doctrinally dangerous manner from God the Father to St Benedict Joseph Labre and enlisted the help of all of them to protect us from 'the temptations of the world, the concupiscence of the flesh, and the pride of life'. We did not question their aptness – nor indeed do I now – for the Lord took it all in his stride and marked us on intention rather than artistic content.

The same might be said of our behaviour in church. We were marshalled into our seat – the same seat in the same row at the same Mass every Sunday, and woe betide anyone who tried to trespass. Similarly, we were marshalled into Confession when we reached the appropriate age, and marshalled up to Communion, and marshalled out again. The only deviations were the unforeseeable events, such as the time I got thrown out of the confession box by the priest, or the time I got lost on the way back from Communion – but that is another story.

The routine was such a part of us, and the Morris Eight was such a part of the routine that when the last verse of the hymn ended with 'Oh could this transport last' I automatically assumed that it was the voice of the universal Church calling on the Almighty to preserve, protect and defend all the other Morris Eights which were just as unreliable and unpredictable as our own.

Life and Love

There is nothing better geared to raising hackles on the neck of every reasonable and right-thinking woman – not to mention the more extreme feminists – than that statement of St Paul that, 'the husband is head of his wife' and consequently 'wives should submit to their husbands in everything'. It generates such passion and occasionally such hatred that the readers rarely go any further and consequently miss the point, that St Paul was not trying to make life more oppressive for women but that within the context of the lifestyle of those days he was trying to ensure that wives were given respect and dignity rather than being treated merely as their husband's property.

No one will deny that throughout history there have been plenty of bad husbands – husbands who degraded their wives, beat them, insulted them, overworked them and rejected them – and throughout history there have been plenty of good husbands – husbands who loved their wives, treasured them, cared for them, delighted in them and stuck with them to the door of death. In our own day there are many good husbands – faithful, caring and thoughtful – but we have allowed ourselves to be conned by a tiny minority of influential communicators into believing that Christian marriage – and various other Christian beliefs – is on its way out; not really geared to life in the twenty-first century; an oppressive framework within which no one can hope to find personal satisfaction and fulfilment.

If you have any doubts about this then ask yourself, when is the last time you saw a film or television programme which showed marriage in a favourable light? How many of the juvenile characters in films and soap operas came from stable, traditional families of father, mother and children? How many happy families can you remember? How many caring and loving fathers and mothers?

The programme makers' defence is:

> We don't shape the world. We merely reflect the situation we find. It's not our fault if traditional marriage is on the slide with one out of every two marriages ending in divorce. It's not our fault that murder, robbery, fraud, rape, incest, sexual abuse, and promiscuity are so prevalent. We didn't create this world. We just reflect it.

Well, lets see just how accurately you reflect it.

Marriage is falling apart, you tell us. In America one in every two marriages ends in divorce; and to prove this point you quote the figures for the year 1981: 2.4 million marriages, 1.2 million divorces, therefore half of all marriages end in divorce.

When I was at school you were slapped, sometimes very severely, for making elementary mathematical mistakes like that. Turn the figures around. Lets say that there were 1.2 million marriages and 2.4 million divorces in 1981. Does that mean that there are twice as many divorces as marriages in America?

Figures have to be treated very carefully. You can prove nearly anything with statistics, especially if you put your answer in percentages. Imagine, for example, you have five happily married women seated around a table. All married; none divorced. And you are asked, 'What is the percentage divorce rate for these people?' You say five people, no divorces, so the percentage rate of divorce is zero. Then you invite, say, the film star Elizabeth Taylor, who has been divorced six times, to join the other ladies at the table, and again you ask what is the percentage divorce rate of these ladies? Well, you now have six married ladies and six divorces so the percentage rate of divorce must be 100 per cent – or is it? Obviously there is something wrong here. The real rate, in fact, is nearer sixteen per cent, but that is the kind of specious argument that is being doled out to us day in, day out, and we accept them and let our lives be guided by them.

We are told that family life is disintegrating. Ask anybody. So we ask anybody, and what do we find. Oh yes, everyone is firmly convinced that other people's family life is in a bad way and other people's marriages are under threat or already falling apart. But what about your own family, we ask, your own marriage? How is it standing up? Oh, my family is doing very well. I have great hopes for them. And my marriage is holding together in spite of all the pressures of modern life.

The same percentage of people who believe that marriage is done for and the family is in danger of disappearing also believe that their own family and their own marriage are in good shape. Now which family and which marriage would the people be likely to know better – their own or someone else's? It is because we have been conditioned by the image makers, the culture shapers of our time, to believe that marriage and the family are a thing of the past, that we imagine that our own marriage and our own family is the only one that is likely to survive. The real number of people who do not want a stable, committed married relationship and who do not believe that children benefit from being brought up in a loving community of father, mother and children is a mere fraction of the whole community. Why should we allow them to dictate the tone and the standards of our moral life, when they represent nobody but themselves.

Not merely have we been deceived into believing that their view of married life is the view of most people. They have also bullied our children into believing that their own warped and sometimes despairing view of sexuality is the view of all liberal-minded and progressive people. Children are pressurised by the images they see and the lifestyles that they imitate into believing that sexual activity is not just a desirable but a mandatory symptom of healthy adolescent life. Children – for many of them are little more than children – should be allowed to live like children and play like children and enjoy their childhood without being pressurised into living and dressing and behaving like diminutive adults. 'Babies having babies' was how Jessie Jackson, the black American politician, described it, and he has seen some of the devastation that these ideas have wrought in his own country among his own people.

I am tempted to quote an American columnist, a woman who reflects the same kind of disapproval as myself of the modern 'liberal' media, but her disapproval is so intense that she is willing to set aside all recent developments in understanding and compassion, and restore a hard-line policy that demands high standards of behaviour, and she doesn't hesitate to publicly shame those who let those standards drop.

A hard line indeed, but if secular newspaper columnists are so appalled by what is happening to marriage and family life surely the Christian churches cannot afford to stand by in silence. Surely it is time we began to fight back.

Media Muscle

You could be easily led to believe nowadays that because your name is in the headlines you must be an important person. Media people are very good at their jobs, very persuasive. When they want an interview they can make you feel absolutely central to the well-being of the human race. But, like the travelling salesman, they move on the next day to a new town and leave a trail of disillusioned devotees in their wake. A lot of people still have to learn that we only get fifteen minutes of fame in this world, and then its back to porridge. We're yesterday's men and women, and only a fool tries to warm up the corpse.

Some years back, a young man of republican persuasion confronted me for not bringing the full weight of the Catholic Church to bear on a particular problem in Magilligan Jail at the time, but it was his follow-up line which really unbalanced me: 'Does the Pope know about this?' he asked. I formed this picture in my mind of the Pope leafing through the pages of the *Derry Journal* or *The Sentinel* looking for the latest developments in the province. It didn't seem too likely. Somehow I did not see the Pope having time to disentangle the knots in the life of Magilligan Jail.

Equally unlikely was the idea of the Pope keeping in personal touch with me about what he was or was not doing. So I told him that the chances were that the problems in Magilligan Jail came way down the priority list after things like genocide in Africa, massacres in East Timor, slavery in the Middle East, oppression of women in India, child abuse everywhere, not to mention earthquake, famine, drought, hurricane or even the odd plague of locusts. He wasn't impressed. 'Well, if he doesn't know, he should know about it,' he snapped.

As a country we've been in the headlines for a long time. Our fifteen minutes have definitely been extended, but we're in grave danger now of being switched off at the plug. Everyone has heard our arguments. They've seen our outrages. They have grown used to our atrocities. We are no longer headline news. We cannot rely on the interest of other people and other nations to motivate our search for a lasting solution to our problems. We have to get down to it together and do the job ourselves; and we have to rethink our reliance on the media. It's worth remembering what the headline writers themselves say, 'If you live by the media, you die by the media.'

Part of the Crowd

'As he stepped ashore, he saw a large crowd: and he took pity on them.'

My own instinct, when I see 'a large crowd' is to run – and run fast – for cover. Crowds have that unhappy knack of being most unpredictable when you are least prepared. They can prowl around the periphery of our lives for years, rather like a pride of domesticated lions, flexing their muscles and yawning disinterestedly, without causing any anxiety, until that fatal day arrives when we make the wrong move or say the wrong word; then we find ourselves fleeing in mystified terror before a fury that we had never imagined.

I have seen a placid crowd of spectators turn into an avenging mob because someone floated an entirely unfounded rumour that a policeman had batoned a pregnant woman, and all of us have seen the mindless carnage that can break loose at apparently peaceful football matches. You do not have to be part of the problem to get caught up in the effects. Sometimes even the crowd does not have to be part of the problem to get caught up in the effects. I wandered round the city of Derry taking photographs, an hour before the fateful march on Bloody Sunday. Everything seemed so boringly normal that eventually I gave up hope of getting any unusual photographs and went home. It was a bitterly cold day anyway, and that helped to make my mind up. But, as we all know, the normality of that crowd was shattered in an instant, and the results have scarred not just a town but a nation for many years.

The crowds that Jesus encountered were fairly typical. They could be selfish, stupid, deceived or stampeded, and always at the level of the most gullible member. They were as strong as the weakest link. The crowd in today's gospel, for example, took no account of the fact that Jesus had just heard of the death of his closest friend, John the Baptist. The crowd on Palm Sunday insisted on escorting him in triumph through the streets of Jerusalem without any reference to Jesus' wishes on the matter, just as that same crowd turned on him on Good Friday and screamed for his death.

No wonder the Apostles, faced with this particular crowd, asked Jesus to 'send the people away'. Most of us would have done the same, but Jesus 'took pity on them', as he takes pity on all of us, for we are part of a crowd. We have the same gullibility, the same emotionalism, the same dependability, the same short-sightedness and the same short memory. We 'spend our wages on what fails to satisfy' and refuse to pay attention to God so that 'our souls will live'. We are the adman's dream, and the prophet's nightmare, for we 'spend our money on what is not bread' and have no time for 'an everlasting covenant'. Jesus fed the crowd, and prepared them for the Eucharist. We have to be enticed gently with the 'bread that perishes', before we learn to hunger for the 'Bread of Life'.

Bonum Est Diffusivum Sui

Goodness always wants to spread itself. That's what I was taught back in the fifties, and it may still be true. Good people do tend to bring out the best in others.

That being so, one might reasonably enquire why the leadership of the Catholic Church is so unwilling to share out its gifts and graces with the rest of the Church. Instead of showering every possible benefit upon the people, it squirrels away its power and its privileges and seems intent on convincing the ordinary squaddies in God's army that everything they possess is a privilege, not a right, and only very important people can be trusted to dispense these privileges in a careful and methodical manner. Open the floodgates to the entire church and all kinds of upstarts from parish councils to bishop's conferences will start demanding the right to make decisions and apply the law. If only …

For example, the Catholic Church is firmly convinced that general absolution of sins lies within its power, but suggests that it should only be used in extremely rare situations. The end of the second millennium seemed to a lot of people a rare situation indeed. In fact, they were predicting that we wouldn't have another for the next thousand years , but it wasn't rare enough for the Vatican. They are going to hang on until something really important crops up.

The ordination of married men is another gift that lies within its power, but while it is willing to make an exception for Anglican ministers who come its way – for whatever reason – it daren't open the floodgates to all the common or garden priests of the Catholic Church who seek the same privilege.

Consider also the situation with marriages today. A hundred years ago every marriage of Catholic and non-Catholic in a non-Catholic Church was accepted as genuine by the Catholic Church, but not since 1903. Suddenly it announced that all Catholics would have to be married before their own priest in their own church, and the non-Catholic parties would have to toe the line. Today it is slowly working its way back to the pre-1903 position, but do not expect any landmark decisions. Every case still has to be examined and approved individually.

Is the Church in some kind of danger from lesser mortals – including bishops – who finally get to exercise freely their prerogatives as children of God, or is there a greater danger from the bureaucrats who cling jealously to their un-christlike exercise of power, and whose only objective seems to be to maintain the status quo – and maybe also their jobs – at whatever the cost?

Tirade

I am aging rapidly. My health is declining, and I have aches and pains as yet to be identified by medical science, as well as a lifetime of sin that needs forgiving, so, with death at least peeking in my direction I have no desire to get into a beef with the Catholic Church or its leaders.

Even so, I cannot in all honesty pass over the epidemic of peripheral devotions that is threatening to engulf the traditional patterns of faith and worship in the Catholic Church. Well in the forefront are all the Marian apparitions that have claimed our attention in the past fifty years. Spain, Egypt, Venezuela, Nicaragua, Argentina, Holland, the Philippines, Bosnia, Syria, South Korea, Ukraine, Ecuador, Arizona, Ohio, Georgia, Illinois, California, China, Russia and Slovakia have all claimed that the Virgin Mary has appeared on their soil with yet another message for the world. Add to these the local apparitions that have flourished for a day and then faded into well-deserved oblivion and we need not be surprised if someone is tempted to launch a second reformation before very long.

Hard on the heels of the apparitions are the novenas and devotions that have mushroomed across the country, invariably touted as 'never known to fail', and we begin to wonder where the Church is heading. Padre Pio's mitt is carried from prayer group to prayer group, in the pious expectation of miracles, even though the man himself had very little time for the kind of people who pursued miraculous solutions to life's problems while the down to earth christians grafted away unnoticed at the service of God and neighbour. I attended his Mass on one occasion and as he walked towards the sacristy at the end of Mass a little old lady – no doubt overflowing with piety and good intentions – rushed from her pew as he passed and grabbed his hand to kiss it. It was probably painful, for the wounds on his hands always looked raw and inflamed, but his reaction took no account of patience or piety. He let what is known in Northern Ireland as a 'gulder' at her and in no uncertain terms told her to return to her seat and stop torturing the clergy. If we add the bones of St Therese, which are currently being trundled around the country, one can only wonder how carefully all these promoters of exotic Christianity have scrutinised the teachings of Vatican II which state in fairly blunt terms: 'Let them carefully refrain from whatever might by word or deed lead the separated brethren or any others whatsoever into error about the doctrine of the Church.'

Even so, there are dedicated supporters of this à la carte Christianity who not merely believe in Lourdes and Fatima and Medjugorje and Knock and who count up their pilgrimages like gamblers counting their winnings, and who are willing to walk, if not run, down the latest ecclesiastical catwalk in pursuit of a saint whose life was dedicated to solitude and silence, while the rest of us sinners battle wearily along the road of tradition and orthodoxy. They will continue to promote their esoteric devotions in the firm belief that if the Pope has given it even half a sentence in one of his many thousands of addresses to his flock this will be sufficient justification for the ecclesiastical enthusiasts to impose it on the rest of us.

While we can find no enthusiasm for the exotic practices of these Christian worshippers, nonetheless we have no desire to place obstacles on their chosen path to God, and while they confine their activities to the privacy of their own hearts and homes we make no objection, but when they carry their liturgical baggage into the local church and create a public disturbance by saying their prayers out loud while the rest of us are keeping the peace, it is time to lodge a protest. It is surely not too much to ask that if they wish to say the rosary, or recite some environmentally friendly composition before Mass they should do so silently and peacefully, to themselves, and realise that we too are entitled to follow our own path to God, especially when all we ask is a brief period of peace and serenity before Mass begins when we hope to have a quiet word with the Almighty.

The Chancellor's Sums

I had to go to Omagh yesterday to take my mother to an eye clinic, and on the journey I gave some deep and philosophic thought to the problem of crime and punishment, or rather, the problem of failure and punishment.

It was all the Chancellor Nigel Lawson's fault. You see, it was the morning of the budget and I had a couple of minutes to spare before starting out and I turned on the television, hoping to get the news, and got instead a sort of political John the Baptist telling me that in a few minutes I would see on my screen Mr Lawson delivering the most important speech of his political life. And, he further informed me that while the generality of mankind might be biting their fingernails with anxiety, in the conservative party confidence was high, in proof of which – and here I think he blew it – he showed us the Prime Minister Mrs Thatcher tripping the light fantastic across the dance floor with Mr Kenneth Baker at the Party Conference. As a public relations exercise I would rate it somewhere below Nero's violin recital the night that Rome burned down. Where I come from this kind of thing is known as 'whistling past the graveyard'.

However, I couldn't wait for Mr Lawson, and on the way to Omagh I pondered deeply, as I said, on the consequences for all of us if Mr Lawson got his sums wrong. You see, where I went to school, if you got your sums wrong you got punished. It didn't matter how hard you had tried or how much time you had spent on your homework, if you got it wrong, you got the hammer along with those who had not tried at all, but the punishment always encouraged you to give it your best shot. However, there was a further wrinkle to punishment in our maths class. You see the teacher used to sit on the front seat in class and tell the boy sitting nearest to him, 'If I get any trouble from anybody, I hit one of you and you can see the culprit outside.' Trouble – like getting your sums wrong – at the back of the class brought swift retribution to the front row.

Now it seems to me that Mr Lawson has got himself a seat at the back of my maths class, and you and I and Joe Public are in the front row. If he gets his sums wrong, we will get it in the neck because the high mortgages and high unemployment and the reduced social services will all land in our direction. And even if, in spite of his highly developed sense of positioning, Mr Lawson should be called to account, he always has his doomsday machine under the desk, the magic manipulator that can change the question to fit the answer – devaluation. If he has to produce twelve pounds he can take twenty pence from each of the ten pounds in your pocket and create two new pounds, and hey-presto, ten plus two equals twelve. The only problem is that the people running the eye clinic may not think that ten of these new pounds are sufficient reward for the work that used to be worth ten old pounds and they may close up shop, and that would not please my mother one little bit, and if I were Mr Lawson I wouldn't get her angry. He does not need the aggro. He has enough trouble as things stand.

Children Without Need

Children have their own way of educating us. I once visited a friend of mine and was met in the doorway by the two-year-old son of the house wearing a pair of green wellies and a cowboy hat, and nothing in between. The front of his Stetson bore the inscription, 'What you sees is what you gets.'

I wonder has anyone ever come up with a better slogan for children than that. What you see is what you get. No pretence, no camouflage, no deception; just the bare unvarnished truth. That is what children naturally give us. Of course, as they grow older, they learn about tact and discretion and manipulation and lying, but for a few delightful years between infancy and the onset of deviousness they are models of sincerity and truth.

Of course, not being used to sincerity and truth we often find their frankness hard to endure. While I may not subscribe fully to the opinion of W. C. Fields that anyone who hates children and dogs cannot be all bad I do agree that children can put you on the most embarrassing spot without batting an eyelid. In a moment of pardonable pride some years back, when I had a rather less rounded figure than I have today, I explained to a young lady of ten – the only audience available at the time – that I could still fit into the cassock which I had worn on ordination day twenty-five years previously. She merely looked me steadily in the eye, completely unimpressed, and asked 'Why? Were you always fat?'

Indeed, I have seen much more patriarchal figures than myself stopped in their tracks by a harmless juvenile. A reverend uncle of mine was standing in the doorway of a farmhouse, bidding goodbye to the farmer's wife after an uplifting pastoral visit, when her four-year-old son ran past trailing a piece of rope behind him. In a ponderous attempt at humour my uncle stood on the rope and brought him to a sharp halt. It was a fatal mistake. Far from being intimidated, the young gentleman merely looked up at him and snapped, 'Get off my rope, you big ...' and I can only tell you that the word he used is not used in polite company.

Now, if your instinct is to reach for a slipper and apply it forcefully to the posterior of these two shining examples of the new generation then be happy, for it is my contention that a happy, healthy child naturally inspires some adults in the vicinity to reach for it by the ear. Only children in need, only the neglected and the sick and the hungry inspire our pity and our tears.

Defeat of Ageism

Have you lately fallen victim to the scourge of ageism in the workplace? In the past we've had racism, nepotism, sexism, favouritism, terrorism, fascism, communism, socialism and conservatism, all messing up our lives one way or another, and now we have ageism, victimisation at work because you do not measure up to the profile of the young and energetic organisation that you work for.

Think about it. You apply for promotion but you're passed over. You are too old. You have worked regularly and successfully in your profession and at forty you are declared redundant. No one wants to rehire you. You are too old. You've taken early retirement with the intention of working part-time but no one wants you. You are too old. Huge numbers of perfectly healthy, capable people are condemned to a life of idleness, boredom and frustration because some high flying yuppie thought they were too old.

Well, weep no more, for help is on the way. I have found a profession where you can be guaranteed full-time employment from the moment you qualify until the day you slide gently into the grave – the Catholic Priesthood. At forty you will be considered a mere youngster on the job. At sixty-five you will be in the prime of life, and at eighty you may even find yourself being asked to choose between a number of new and exciting positions. The situation is so critical in fact and the number of vacancies so great that even compulsory retirement at seventy-five is inevitably followed by a request that you continue where you left off.

Redundancies are unknown in this line of work, and eccentricity is no barrier to promotion. If you have the basic qualifications, we have the work. Of course, that can be a problem because there is no training on the job. You have to spend up to seven years learning the business and you have to take whatever job they give you. Your personal life can take a hammering too because you can be transferred to a branch office fifty miles from home at a week's notice. The hours are unpredictable and the demands of the customers can be a bit excessive. In some places you can be roused from your bed by dedicated patrons of the alcohol business who have found God at three o'clock in the morning and want to know what to do with Him. Your domestic bliss may be curtailed by the fact that romantic unions, either same-sex or different, are both banned – at least for the present. But solitude has much to commend it. In short, the job profile may be a bit weird but you can work forever. Even our Chief Executive is in his eighties and he has no notion of quitting.

Fear and Faith

'Man of little faith, why did you doubt?'

There is an old abandoned gold-mining town in New Zealand called Skippers that can only be reached by a one-lane dirt road that winds its way around the contours of a very steep hillside. It is part of the tourist trap nowadays, and adventurous motorists regularly tackle the journey without any qualms or hesitation. If you are a passenger, however, as I was, you notice that the driver tends to grip the steering wheel more tightly, and to blink a lot less, as the journey progresses. There is the definite feeling that even one mistimed blink could send both car and occupants over the precipice, so conversation dies and blood pressure rises. By the time the driver has finished the ten- or twelve-mile journey, he is emotionally drained, so that when he has viewed the mineshafts and the scattered tombstones of 'natives of Ireland' and wondered at the presence of a telephone on a nearby pole, and is finally ready to go home, he suddenly finds that his nerve has gone, and he can no longer even think of starting the return journey. It is as though his entire nervous system has frozen up. He cannot move. (At this point the telephone begins to make sense). He eventually joins that growing band of mortified travellers who have had to endure the double indignity of being driven back to civilization in one car while their own car is driven behind them by someone else.

'Man of little faith, why did you doubt?' asked Jesus of Peter, and the answer is, 'Because I was frightened out of my wits. Because I couldn't risk letting go.' It will happen to all of us eventually. We will lose our nerve and not even God will persuade us to let go.

And it will happen a lot nearer home than New Zealand. A clerical colleague in a moment of madness, climbed on to the roof of his church where workmen were repairing the ridge tiles – and froze. No amount of persuasion or assurance could prise his hands loose. It took a rescue team with ropes three hours to get him back on to the ground.

Faced with the shock of sudden bereavement or fatal illness or even the enormity of our sins, we realise the futility of our own efforts, and freeze up. We have not yet acquired the courage to take the hand of Jesus and to follow him wherever he leads us. God is indeed found in 'the gentle breeze', but I believe that we have to come through the fire and the earthquake and the mighty wind before we find him. We have to get ducked in the waters of the lake a couple of times before we begin to believe in the gentle power of Jesus. We have to get bashed about a few times by the forces of life before we can turn to Jesus and say 'truly you are the Son of God'. We have to be scared out of our wits a few times before we can trust the words, 'Courage, it is I. Do not be afraid.' We have to stand shivering a few times on the brink of death before we can say, 'Into your hands I commit my spirit.'

How to Be a Failure –
Without Really Trying

Unless or until you have been a fat teenager you can have no idea of what is meant by adolescent failure. If, in addition, you are a fat teenager wearing hand-me-down clothes, then you have no need to wait for disaster. You are a walking disaster. Everything about you screams to the heavens that you have failed in the most fundamental objectives of teenage life. You are neither 'swinging', 'groovy', 'trendy', 'laid-back', 'with it' nor 'cool'.

Let me try to dissect this calamity into its component parts. Firstly, I was born into an age of comfortable fattiness. There were no hang-ups about carbohydrates or cholesterol. A fat baby was a healthy baby, and since skinniness was a sign of either poverty or neglect, a conscientious mother did all in her power to build up her offspring until he took on the dimensions of a sumo wrestler.

I was not aware that I had become the victim of this freewheeling – if false – gastronomic theory until I had spent some time at school. There I ran into a couple of down-to-earth critics – straight from the pages of the Beano, with their prickly haircuts and roll-top jerseys – who informed me bluntly that I was not merely a fatty but a curly-top as well. No greater insult could be offered to an incipient man-of-the-world so I foolishly – very foolishly, as it turned out – demanded satisfaction, and got a various left jab to the nose that left me fat, curly and bleeding.

I never really got over my hang-ups about fatness, even in boarding school, where survival became a priority and fatness merely a hopeful dream. I made the mistake of confusing weight with overweight, and my worst fears were confirmed when, at the age of fourteen, all the students were subjected to a compulsory medical examination. One of the less grisly aspects of the examination was having our weight recorded, and when I stepped on the scales and registered eleven solid stones there were muffled gasps of shock? Astonishment? Embarrassment? I'm not sure which, and they did not ease anything when the next in line took to the scales and turned out to be a six-stone weakling.

This crisis led on in due course to the next phase of my calamity. Fashion was not a popular word in those days, because you needed coupons as well as money to buy clothes, and most of us had neither. There was, however, a style-of-the-day in men's overcoats – the trench coat. Everyone went around looking like Humphrey Bogart. You couldn't find a blank bit of wall but there was a young fellow leaning up against it, wearing a trench coat and his da's hat, and nearly blinding himself with the cigarette smoke that curled into one eye as he tried to look tough.

I had no trench coat. In fact I had no coat at all, for I had outgrown the coat I used to have, and off-the-peg models that fitted me were hard to find. Besides, my mother was a very thrifty woman and she had a brainwave that would save money, provide me with a coat, and make sure it was not a trench coat – of which she did not approve – all at the same time. She took down my father's wedding – or rather, his honeymoon – coat from the closet where it had lain in mothballs for years and got a local tailor to shorten it. Not too much, you understand, for in those days you always made allowance for growth. For example, a new pair of trousers were expected to reach your armpits on the grounds that one day you might grow into them.

Anyway, the amended overcoat was duly rolled out – and I almost cried when I saw it. In fact, I think I did cry. It was the most hideous overcoat I have ever seen – dark brown, absolutely straight from top to bottom, with padded shoulders. When I put it on I looked like a cross between a Sephardic Jew and a Chicago gangster. Needless to say, the trench coat brigade went into hysterics when they saw it. Their most charitable comment was that if I lived long enough the fashion might make a comeback.

The awful irony was that they were right. I met my niece in town the other day. She was wearing a coat that was the mirror image of my dark brown calamity; and, I need hardly say, she is a very fashion-conscious young lady.

Latest News From the Eighties

The American lady who said, in a television interview, that she thought Christmas was a wonderful thing – that they really ought to have it every year, wasn't so wide of the mark as one might think. The basic Christmas event, the birth of Christ, has in fact disappeared from most of our seasonal greetings, and I suppose, after all, if we can get around to thinking that God is dead we should have no trouble getting around to the idea that Christmas is cancelled.

All this came to me in a fairly rapid revelation when the man from the BBC said, 'I'd like you to do a news review, but with Christmas in mind.' It sounded easy – just collect all the references and attitudes to Christmas from the newspapers, and pass a profound judgment on them. The only problem was that the newspapers had other things on their mind, and had for the most part completely overlooked Christmas. The commercial end of the papers were full of suggestions for Christmas presents, and the advertisements all had the obligatory Santa Claus hawking his wares, but there was a boring sameness about it all. Previously they had urged us to buy their double-sprocket-multicore-hydrostatic cement mixer. Now they urged us to buy Granny or Mother-in-law or great aunt Nellie a double-sprocket-multicore-hydrostatic cement mixer for Christmas.

The only thing I could find with a Christmassy flavour was an article on how to plan your Christmas dinner, backed up by some seventeenth-century advice on table manners, and a treatise on parthenogenesis. Now if you had the misfortune to be saddled with what was laughingly called 'a classical education' you will know the meaning of that big word. If, on the other hand, you had a useful education you will be intrigued to hear that it means virgin birth. It merits discussion in our newspapers more on scientific than religious grounds, but editors are not averse to setting the two down together if they think it makes a headline. In this instance they tell us that certain fish, lizards, bees and turkey eggs can reproduce without so much as a squiggle from a sperm, but the learned conclusion is that, leaving aside any divine intervention, a human foetus reproduced in the same way would finish up dead before it was born, carrying a hereditary disease and female. That last item has to do with X and Y genes – about which I know nothing – but apparently any natural brand of virgin-birth is going to carry female genes only.

The article on management of the Christmas dinner was equally rare, though slightly more intelligible. It asks 'Have you organised your campaign as thoroughly as a military manoeuvre?' and assuming that you have not – very wisely, I would say – it tells you how to get things in shape so that 'you will have time to open presents with the family, have a drink with seldom-seen relations, or even get to church'. Maybe it's my old-fashioned upbringing, but that last one – 'even getting to church' – struck me as hilarious. It's a bit like telling a bride how to organise her wedding, with the afterthought that she might even have time to get married. It continues with hints about surreptitiously inserting coins into the Christmas pudding – can't you just see half a dozen children choking on brass pounds, or spitting out bits of broken teeth – and then concludes with safety-conscious instructions on how to open the champagne without putting out someone's eye.

The seventeenth-century advice on etiquette was far more down to earth. It urged you not to 'blow your nose at the table without holding your hat before your face' nor 'to claw your head, to belch, to hawk or tear anything up from the bottom of your stomach'. That kind of thing was definitely lower-class.

The BBC had a big ad for its books, which concentrated heavily on food too. We had Michael Smyth's *New English Cookery*, Delia Smith's *Complete Cookery Book*, *Floyd on Fish*, *The Taste of Health*, and ominously followed, I thought, by *Going to Pot* and finishing up with *The Day the Universe Changed*. This staggering emphasis on food is going to puzzle sociologists in centuries to come when they try to fit Christmas eating habits into any rational plan of twentieth-century behaviour. I have visions of a little green man from planet Upsilon Sigma two thousand years hence writing a thesis on planet Earth's Christmas celebrations. 'December of each year', it should run, 'was devoted to celebrating the great consumer festival. It culminated in a sacred dinner on the 25 December when families gathered together and donned the traditional headgear before sitting down to a meal consisting of the same ingredients each year, cooked and presented according to longstanding and rigorously enforced regulations. A strange and rather ruthless precaution was always taken to ensure that large amounts of these ingredients would do no lasting medical damage. In the weeks prior to the dinner the older members of the society were transported to regional centres where they were compelled to eat huge quantities of these same ingredients, and were afterwards subjected to intense levels of tobacco smoke and electronic noise, presumably in the belief that if the older and weaker members of the tribe could survive this ordeal it would be unlikely to cause any great discomfort to the young and healthy.' Or maybe he will figure it was a conservation festival – what with all the dogs and cats and reindeers and little red robins that we see on Christmas cards – though now I think of it, he might run into problems with all those dead turkeys.

However, we cannot blame the newspapers for all this. They merely reflect, rather than create, our image. Everyone is an honorary Christian at Christmas, just as all New Yorkers are honorary Irishmen on St Patrick's Day, and where they drink green beer to proclaim their allegiance, we eat turkey and Christmas pudding to proclaim ours, and since that is the depth of our Christianity, small wonder that we find little trace of it in our newspapers.

'A fat person with poor dress-sense –
a large and very stupid bird –
a zany story – small explosive devices –
what can it all mean?'

Leni Riefenstahl

The writer John Steinbeck was so caught up in his craft that a friend said he would sell his own grandmother for a good story. Steinbeck's response was that a good story was worth any number of little old ladies, a literary judgement that you may find hard to reject, unless of course you happen to be a little old lady.

Good writers are not necessarily nice people. I know a man who was familiar with the poet Paddy Kavanagh and he said he was an awful man especially when drunk, but he wrote *The Great Hunger*.

Dylan Thomas was rarely anything but drunk but he wrote:

Do not go gentle into that good night,
rage, rage at the dying of the light.

You can forgive a man with that kind of genius for taking a drink.

Painters and poets, sculptors and composers, novelists and designers, all have been accepted for their genius, even though they fitted badly into the world around them. But somehow the artistic and intellectual world seems unwilling to accept the faults and limitations of Leni Riefenstahl, who died the other day at the age of 101.

Most of you probably never heard of her, but in the pre-Second World War period she was the most famous documentary film maker in the world, and this at a time when film was the ultimate entertainment medium. Her most famous films were *Triumph of the Will*, an account of the rise to power of Hitler, and *Olympia*, the record of the 1936 Berlin Olympics. Both these films won awards all over the world, and even as late as 1937 *Triumph of the Will* was given the top prize at the French Art Exhibition. Until the Second World War started she was recognised as a genius by world critics but once the murderous nature of Hitler's regime began to reveal itself she became an outcast in the film business. When she was at her peak her rivals envied her, but they all wanted to know her. They were only too happy to be seen with this beautiful and brilliant woman who had the ear and the admiration of Adolf Hitler, even though she had the unqualified hatred of Joseph Goebbels.

But the war changed all that. Her work was vilified by the allies as fascist Nazi propaganda. She could get no work in the film business for many years after the war. Her critics said she was 'artistically a genius and politically a nitwit', so in a strange inversion of the sin and the sinner proverb they loved her creations and hated their creator.

I've never had much time for those people who tell me that they hate the sin but love the sinner. In my experience the sinner usually takes a few hard knocks from his critics before the argument is ended. If we can accept every other artistic creator who ever wrote a great poem or composed a great symphony or painted a great picture, we should be able to accept a director who has made a great film and we should be able to live with the personal and political limitations of the likes of Leni Riefenstahl.

Lest We Forget

As I slowly, but steadily, sink into the depths of clerical senility, I regret that I did not keep a diary of the daily doings and disasters of the priestly life. If, at any stage, I felt a dim fluttering of guilt for not recording the more significant events, I have always excused myself on the grounds that when I had the leisure time to maintain a diary nothing of interest was happening, and when my world was submerged in lunacy and danger I had no time to worry about diaries.

I should have made time. The diaries would have reminded me of the things I have forgotten – and I am constantly amazed at how much I have forgotten that others have remembered – and they would have also confirmed and verified the things that I think I have remembered. Experience has taught me how dangerous it is to rely on memories of forty years ago.

Nonetheless, we lived in such tumultuous times that we should not allow them to be forgotten. We tend to forget how abnormal life was because we were dedicated to keeping things normal – to maintaining the routine of Masses and baptisms and weddings and funerals – while the insanity of death and destruction continued unabated around us.

Looking back, it can almost seem hilarious. Where else but the Longtower Parish in Derry would you be roused from your bed at 2.30 a.m. by a seriously intoxicated couple and asked to give them a lift to Shantallow – and where else would a parish priest finish up doing just that. My biggest problem, I recall, was getting them out of the car, for they began fighting as soon as they got into the back seat.

Death, however, was not hilarious. There were too many deaths; vicious deaths, cruel deaths, unnecessary deaths; too many frenzied denunciations, fabricated statements, pretentious condemnations. Everyone had an unassailable justification for killing and maiming, but the rest of us merely saw mangled corpses and the shattered families.

I grew up during the Second World War. I thought life was perfectly normal then. The present generation must be reminded again and again that the recent history of this country was anything but normal.

Lying Labels

'Even house dogs can eat the scraps that fall from their master's table.'

It was told of the late Cardinal Heenan that at his first press conference as Archbishop of Westminster, when asked by the reporters where he would like to begin, he suggested that they begin with the period of his life when he was a pagan. This answer, naturally, sent them scurrying for their notepads, but the pace fell off sharply when he pointed out to them that it had been for a very brief period in his early life, and had been brought to a speedy end by infant Baptism. Presumably, the reporters were so used to labels defining each aspect of life that the introduction of a new label to describe a period which they were already familiar with threw them off balance. The attitude is not new. Most of us expect everything to have a label and we expect the label to conform to the Trades Description Act, whether on the spiritual or the temporal level. If the label attached to the coat says 'linen', we expect the coat to be linen, and we demand the protection of the law from anyone who would dare to proclaim as linen what is merely cotton. If the label says 'Christian', we automatically extend our expectations, and look for the more obvious Christian virtues, in anyone who wears the label.

Our expectations are shaped by our experiences. If a new label is stuck on the latest pain-killing compound, leading us to believe that it will eradicate our pain in a way that all others have failed to do, a brief acquaintance soon tells us that it is merely another variation of the old reliable, aspirin or paracetamol. A new label is stuck on the latest 'Christian' religion which turns out to be nothing more than a rearrangement of some wholesome humanistic principles, such as saving the ecology, being kind to animals, campaigning for nuclear disarmament or giving, in moderation, to the deserving poor – and all of them flavoured with a sprinkling of godliness.

We expect labels to be informative, but they are often merely confusing. We have to start transferring our attention from the label to the contents. A small boy of nine taught me this lesson very sharply, not so long ago. He came from the worst kind of home – a strong-minded mother for whom money and pleasure were the only realities, and a weak but loving father. He was treated abominably by his mother. He was beaten, deprived, sneered at, threatened, frightened, and humiliated in public. After many years, the father finally found strength to tackle the problem and applied for a divorce, and won complete custody of his child. He later ran into a good woman, whom he had known before his marriage, who befriended the child and helped him to recover some of his self-respect. On his own initiative the child took to calling this woman 'mother' – referring to the natural mother simply as 'that woman who used to live with us', and gave a crushingly simple explanation for his behaviour. A mother, he said, was someone who loved her children, who cared for them and treated them kindly. His natural mother had done none of these things so she had no right to the title of mother. The other woman had done all these things, so henceforth she would be his mother.

The label of 'Christian' is not enough. The old tale of the man who stood trial for being a Christian and was found not guilty is alarmingly relevant today.

Animals and Attitudes

I should be an expert on animals – at least on farm animals – because I spent most of my youth looking after them. Cattle, sheep and pigs were the standard items; occasionally we might branch off into geese, goats and even ponies, but cattle and sheep were the bread-and-butter stock. If the cattle took sick you were in serious trouble; for whether, in those days, there were any benefits available to the poor and the unfortunate, did not matter to us. In our house, if the animals died we tightened our belts.

Now to most of us one cow looks very much like another cow. If one is black and the other is white we might distinguish them, but if they are both red and both about the same size we are likely to run into problems, but not so the farmer or the dealer. To him they are all individuals, and like individuals some are good-looking and some are what James Thurber used to describe as 'homely'. Some are healthy and some are delicate, but since the farmer's ultimate object is to get as good a price as possible for his stock, he didn't hesitate in days gone by to follow human practice and dress them up to look well in the market place.

Some of his methods were quite acceptable. If the animal looked a bit bony he would brush the hair back up against the grain to make it look sturdier and fatter. Other tactics were a bit more questionable. It was not unknown for farmers to mix a liberal sprinkling of salt into the animal's feed before market day, so that it would drink plenty of water on the morning in question and add substantially to its size and its weight. It was not unlike the method practiced by shady car dealers in days gone by of putting a dose of heavy sludge, or even a minced up nylon stocking, into the engine to give it a smoother sound.

The problem with tactics such as these is that they represent bad marketing by any standards, for they do damage to both buyer and seller. Are you likely to deal again with someone who has sold you a car that breaks down after a week on the road or a cow that shrinks to a skeleton the next day? A good reputation counts for a lot in the market place, and also in the heart of man – we all need the respect of others – and a good reputation before God counts for no less, especially if we keep in mind that if we have done some sharp practice to the least of our brethren, we have done it to the Lord Himself.

Lord, let me not be too clever in my dealings with my fellow men today. Let me realise that it is more important to me, and more beneficial, to earn their respect rather than to exploit their ignorance.

Maybe the Old Ways

I have five nursing homes in my parish so the question of looking after elderly parents is a fairly familiar one, not to mention the fact that I have a ninety-one-year-old mother who requires a fair bit of care and attention.

It has been my experience, though I can't prove that it is true for everyone, that the children who received the toughest upbringing are the most conscientious in looking after elderly parents. One lady told me recently that when she was a child her mother said to her – presumably at the climax of some fairly trenchant argument about what she could or could not do – 'I don't care if I have to go to jail for it' – and this was long before the cane ceased to be an integral part of every household – 'while you live in this house you will show me respect and obedience because I am your mother.'

That woman has visited her now paralysed mother every day for the past three years and would cheerfully take her home and care for her by herself if she thought for one moment that she could improve her condition or extend her life for even one minute.

Today's buzz words are 'fulfilment', 'freedom' and 'personal independence', and it's not working. Everyone is afraid of being 'judgmental', of imposing their ideas and standards on others. Everyone wants to be neutral, to allow others – and that includes children – to develop their own standards as though goodness were simply the natural result of allowing everyone – and especially children – to do what they want. The consequence of this approach has been a nine hundred per cent rise in the crime rate for Northern Ireland over the past fifty years. Even the most broadminded liberal must surely wonder if maybe the time has come to introduce some kind of deterrent.

I recently attended a conference on suicide and one of the speakers said quite bluntly, 'the fear of hell and eternal damnation kept a lot of people from committing suicide. They felt they couldn't risk the consequences.'

Maybe it is time to reintroduce some tough measures. Maybe there is even a place in our culture for punishment. Children who had a tough upbringing learned about respect and obedience from their homes and they learned very clearly that if you step out of line you will be punished, one way or another.

Good manners and considerate behaviour didn't just come natural to them. They had to be learned and put into practice and cultivated until their responses became instinctive. Maybe it is time for everyone, and that includes the media which has done so much to promote the false doctrine of natural goodness, to take stock of the situation and start popularising ideas about sacrifice, discipline and consideration for others.

Read the Instructions

There was a trend some years ago among charismatic Christians and other religious high-flyers of looking for an answer to the increasingly complex problems of modern life by slicing open the Bible at random. It was a sort of sanitised version of Gideon's fleece – which, you may remember, he left out on the front lawn all night to see if the dew would settle on it and give him the green light for starting a war.

I have no report on the success rate of the Bible-slicing procedure. It may indeed have worked for some, but I would think that the chances of finding the appropriate solution to your personal problems would be about the same as dealing yourself a straight flush in a game of poker. After all, if you treat the Bible like a pack of cards, you have no right to expect any better odds.

For myself, I have stuck to the old-fashioned method of dealing with books. I start at the beginning and work my way through. As a means of solving life's problems, I am afraid I cannot recommend it. Far from providing me with answers, the Bible seems to furnish me with a few extra problems every time I open it.

Take, for example, the very first chapter of the very first book, Genesis, where we are told that God created the earth and the animals and the plants and the people and found them all to be very good. Now, I am not disputing God's judgment in this matter, but if they are so good why do I have all these problems with them? I cannot even get the plants to cooperate with me. I want ivy to grow up the gable of my house and instead it grows along the ground. I want moss and lichen to grow on my drystone wall but where does it grow? On the roof of my house. I set rhododendron bushes around the front of my house and they die, but my neighbour tries every device known to man to kill them off his farm and what happens? They jump the fence and invade yet another field.

The animal kingdom is no better behaved. I have a pair of goats who would eat, I was assured, every thorn, briar and benweed in my back garden. They did not eat the thorns and the briars and the benweeds. They risked life and limb by jumping the four-foot fence I had built around my back garden and ate the cypress trees which I had grown, with much difficulty, around the front of my house. I gave the rabbit population of the neighbourhood unrestricted access to my back garden for the purposes of setting up house and rearing families. Where did they start digging the foundations? In my only flower bed at the front of the house.

As for the men and women whom God created in his own image and likeness, I am afraid they have turned out to be a big disappointment, both to me and God. His specifications said that they should love one another, forgive one another, feed one another if they were hungry and shelter one another if they were homeless, but at the latest count, I am told there are forty-six different wars going on around the world at this very moment, and there are 18 million people starving in Africa, not to mention homeless children of six years of age sleeping in the streets of Calcutta.

Either somebody has been messing about with God's handbook, or else He has a very strange idea of what is good. On reflection, the first seems the more likely explanation. We have been disregarding the instruction book, and as a result His creations have all gone astray. If the ivy and the mosses are being gassed by exhaust fumes it is hardly surprising that they try to keep out of the way. If God designed the rhododendron bushes specifically for the Himalayan foothills maybe he did not intend them to set up house in Derry. Maybe the goats are trying to compensate for all the hedgerows and bushes that we chopped down in the name of economy and efficiency, and maybe the rabbits are just trying to set up house near a salad supermarket that does not taste so much of pesticide.

Now, if we get it wrong with plants and animals, all of whom lead a relatively simple life, it is hardly surprising that we have fouled up the plan for the human species as well. If the seas retaliate by refusing to grow any fish when we spill oil all over them, and if the deserts take off in a sandstorm because we drive heavy tanks all over them, we can expect ordinary people to complain when we carry off the forests and the minerals from their countries and give them nothing in return. Maybe it is time to go back to the ultimate handbook and find out what we really should be doing – and not by slicing it open at random. If the Bible contains God's plan, laid down over thousands of years, for the salvation of the human race, I am sure he would like us to get an overall view of it rather than take random snippets from here and there. If we foul up the machinery because we do not read the instructions we can hardly blame God for it.

Repentance Required

The joyful smile on the face of Clare Short and her son as they were reunited after thirty years has probably done more to lift the hearts of adopted men and women throughout the country than all the legislation on the subject for the past century. It was almost a declaration of independence by the adopted. 'We are no longer prisoners of pretence. We are free at last.'

Sadly, such examples are the exception rather than the rule. In the past adoption could often be a cruel and heartless business made under pressure and the threat of abandonment. Some mothers did indeed make a careful and realistic analysis of the situation and conclude that putting the child up for adoption was the right thing to do, but far too many were pressured into parting with their babies just to keep up appearances and the pretence of respectability. The lengths to which some parents – especially fathers – went to conceal the birth of their daughter's illegitimate child were unbelievable.

Some bundled their daughters onto a mailboat to England and escorted them to a hostel or a home where they were left to themselves, without friends, without sympathy, without hope, until the child was born. Then it was an undignified scramble to dispose of this inconvenient child, to make it disappear and allow things to get back to normal. The feelings of the mother, the sense of loss, of betrayal, were brutally disregarded, and she was expected to return home with a smile on her face as though nothing had happened. For those who couldn't carry it off an even worse fate awaited. Postnatal depression was conveniently diagnosed as schizophrenia or some other form of mental illness and the mother was signed into a mental hospital by her parents and quickly forgotten or even abandoned.

Who was to blame for all this? What kind of monster could be so heartless as to do these things?

There were no monsters. Just ordinary people, led astray by pride and prejudice and the arrogance which says, 'We know best.'

Parents were to blame – especially fathers – for putting their pride and their respectability before the welfare of their children. The Church was to blame for reinforcing that pride by insisting that sexual sins were the ultimate degradation when Christ himself taught that love was the greatest commandment. The professionals were to blame – the doctors and the lawyers and the servants of the state – because they collaborated in the conspiracy to cover things up, to pretend that nothing had happened. And the awful tragedy, the ultimate irony was that it deceived no one. In a country area especially, everyone knew. They just didn't talk about it.

Adoption is a marvellous thing for childless couples as I know from the experience of my own family and my own friends, but it should never have happened that mothers were pressured – as so many were – into putting their children up for adoption. The Church and the State and all the other people who did this need to ask their forgiveness.

Rising with the Right Body

'The Almighty has done great things for me.'

I went back to one of the parishes of my youth recently to bury a good woman who spoilt all the priests that came her way. She convinced us that we were all special, and while we were quite happy to accept her judgment on a personal level, we wondered that she found so much to admire in all the other incompetents who crossed her path. In fact, it was her cheerful acceptance and support of what can only be described as 'some right lunatics' in the clerical field that convinced us of her genuine holiness. All of which has very little to do with my subject, but she deserved a eulogy, and she was the occasion of opening my eyes a little wider to one of the more important mysteries of the faith.

I had served in the parish twenty-five years ago, and as I stood outside the wake house trying to put names to the faces that passed me by, I noticed a balding, middle-aged man looking at me with more than average interest. I searched my memory for recognition, but it was a complete blank. For maybe five minutes I watched him out of the corner of my eye, and it was only when he started to walk towards me that everything fell into place. The face, the name, all came back to me from twenty-five years ago. I had known him well. He had not changed very much. A little fatter, a lot balder, the teeth had begun to brown, but it was the same face, the same oblique stance, the same voice. Why had I taken so long to recognise him?

I was suddenly aware that I had cracked the problem of Mary Magdalen and the disciples at Emmaus and the Apostles by the sea of Tiberias. It was only right and proper that they should have difficulty in recognizing the risen Christ. If twenty-five years could make recognition difficult, then certainly the lapse between time and eternity would make it even more so. And yet, there eventually was recognition.

Body and soul belong together because they both make up this particular person, and an immortal soul in isolation is nothing less than a 'lost' soul, wandering eternity in search of the body that was its home. This being so, a glorified body makes sense. The resurrection makes sense. The assumption of Mary makes sense, for if the body of Mary was preserved undefiled from the worldly corruption around her, then surely she must be preserved from the bodily corruption of death, and be reunited immediately with the glorified body that was hers and hers alone. She must be the same Mary, recognisable in eternity as she was on earth, preserved from the fate of us original sinners in eternity, as she was preserved from our fate in life here below.

St Therese and the Bonemobile

The past week has taught me two things. One, that fat baldy priests should not appear on television, even with the best of intentions, and two, that the visit of St Therese's bones is not an unalloyed blessing. In fact, it is probably a big mistake.

Whatever about the wisdom of hiring the Irish Army as pall-bearers, there will always be doubts attached to the propriety of carting St Therese's bones around the country in a plastic bone-mobile, since we have no means of reassuring ourselves that the casket does in fact contain bones and that they are the true bones of St Therese. Incidentally, the question arises, 'Are these all of her bones, or are they only a selection?' I ask this because it has been suggested to me – no doubt by militant, atheistic communists, or rather, straightforward militant atheists since the poor communists have almost disappeared – it has, as I say, been suggested to me that this is merely a token selection of bones and that there is another casket, or indeed several other caskets, containing alternative selections of St Therese's bones doing the rounds of other countries and drawing equally big or even bigger crowds than ourselves. This unfeeling suggestion may stem from the fact that an English orchestra – I can't remember their name – was guilty of a similar offence when it was advertised to appear in two places at once. Apparently they had been pursuing this practice for many years, using temporary musicians to fill the gaps, until finally they found themselves playing in neighbouring towns, with consequent unhappiness on the part of the music lovers. This is not to be confused with multiple appearances of shows like

Riverdance which make no bones, if you'll excuse the pun, about staging a show in London while another company is doing the needful in New York. In any case I am sure it's all spiteful malevolence on the part of the communists, or atheists, this suggestion that there may be another casket or caskets of bones. At least, I do hope it is.

The propriety of using military muscle to transport the casket – be they volunteers or conscripts – has been called into question by all fair-minded citizens, though you must give the soldiery credit for spotting a good public-relations opportunity and making the most of it. Therese's military connections belong to an artificial age of social snobbery and military glory – the horrors of the Somme and Burma and Buchenwald were still to come – and can hardly be quoted as a justification for lining up a group of modern squaddies to carry her coffin. We have all seen too many paramilitary funerals to feel at all happy with uniformed pall-bearers and flag-laden supporters – not to mention the dubious motivation that carries its grief out onto the streets for others to admire. In times of real bereavement most of us want to disappear into a corner and pull the ceiling down after us.

However, let's assume that the motives of the organisers are genuine and that they aim at convincing as many people as possible to venerate these relics. One man suggested in interview that before it is all over two million people will have venerated the relics. And? And nothing. That's it. That's as far as this thing has been thought through. People are looking for God we are told but they are abandoning the institutional Church in droves so let's get St Therese's relics to draw them all back again. Wonderful. Two million people come to kiss the plastic cover over the casket containing Therese's bones. They are searching for God and this is what we give them. The same two million could have joined in the offering of the Body and Blood of Christ to God the Father in the Mass the day before, but they preferred a miraculous answer to the problems of life. They have touched the magic box, and Therese will therefore come to their rescue.

It is so sad. Therese was such a fascinating saint. She knew nothing about the world. She lived in a completely artificial environment but she brought her faith to bear one hundred per cent and she transformed it into a victorious campaign. And I am sure lip service will be paid to her virtues but her followers want to see the casket and touch the bones. That's where it will start and finish for most people.

In fact, the leadership of the Church is flowing with the tide and failing to take a stand on this important issue. Thirty and more years ago, the Church went to a great deal of trouble to lay out the true Catholic Doctrine for all to see and in the Constitution on the Church at the Vatican Council it said to 'let them carefully refrain from whatever might by word or deed lead the separated brethren or any others whatsoever into error about the doctrine of the Church'. And that quotation was made in relation to devotion to the Blessed Virgin. The question has to be asked whether this roadshow is giving a true or false impression of Catholic Doctrine to the non-Catholic people of Northern Ireland? To my mind it is merely adding another weight to the already drowning body of Catholicism and pretending that running around in circles is some kind of rescue operation. There has been no real effort ever in the past thirty years to correct the aberrations that have been moulded and manipulated into the frame of the Church until they now appear as essential and integral parts of Church teaching to every passer-by. When is the last time someone said 'Neither Lourdes nor Fatima nor Medjugorje nor any of the hundreds of apparitions that have been claimed in the past thirty years have any validity in the eyes of the Catholic Church. It is your basic right not merely to reject all these events but also to have your decision respected by every other catholic, especially those in charge.' But that is not happening. In present Catholic culture it is treason to reject Lourdes and outrageous pride to expect sympathy. And yet the fact remains that the revelations of Lourdes like all the other revelations are a private matter between the visionary and God. If we choose to follow them it is entirely our own choice.

The Good Old Days!

As the years hurtle past my big regret is that, like Lord Reith, I never really understood that 'life is for living'. There was always more work to be done, more lessons to be learned, more rules to be obeyed, so that one was always looking forward to better days ahead. Perhaps that is what teachers experience as they wait for Friday, but Friday does eventually come and you can see a spring to their step on a Friday afternoon that is not there on a Monday morning.

Friday should have the same effect on the pupils, but in my school days Friday was a day of reckoning, a day of judgement, a *Dies Irae*, a day of wrath. Friday meant Friday tests, weekly written examinations in mathematics. Six sums in forty-five minutes, with a threat of punishment to keep your mind focused. The exercise books were stacked on the principal's desk and corrected over the weekend. If you got a sum wrong you got so many slaps, so you had the whole weekend to worry about your performance and to anticipate the pain.

I think my generation is still worrying. There was so much fear, so much stress, so much uneasiness. But, then, the teachers were not the only culprits. The Church laid a burden of guilt and shame on everyone's shoulders that took all the joy out of life, in its well-meaning but misguided attempt to keep us all out of trouble, but often the trouble we kept out of was a poor compensation for the trouble we got into.

We grew up waiting for Friday when we would lay down our burden and begin to enjoy life, but instead Friday brought its own burdens; and gradually life passed us by. Today's youth carries a different set of burdens, but 'life is still for living'. It should not be put off until tomorrow. If the joy of life today is overlooked or disregarded it is a joy lost forever.

Now I am far from advocating any kind of reckless or dissolute lifestyle. Nothing could be further from my mind, for nothing is more depressing than a life of sin, but the good in every day should be lived and enjoyed to the full, for there is nothing more plaintive or pathetic than the querulous voice of an old man rehearsing yet again a lament for his lost youth.

The Handbag

My friend Annie died very suddenly. She passed out of this life without time for more than a hurried goodbye to her children and grandchildren and the few friends who lived nearby. She did not die of old age, for in her eyes, her eighty-six years were merely a number which others used to measure the span of her life. She was still young because she felt young, and life was there to be lived and enjoyed, not to be measured out in spoonfuls according to the expectations of some medical or social expert. She did not lie submissively on her bed awaiting the arrival of death. She forced him to pursue her through the town and to scurry after her until finally his cold hand rested on her shoulder and announced that it was time to go.

The curtains of her bedroom window were drawn across the broad lazy river that flowed below her house, and her daughter and I sat in silence beside her coffin and remembered the past. The events of her life rolled by us like a silent news reel – no commentary, no music, no voices, just silent pictures. And then, as though from a distance, I heard her daughter say, 'I have to open her handbag.' For a moment the words meant nothing to me. What was important about a handbag? Suddenly I remembered. The days of my childhood and my mother's handbag, that sacred treasury of her innermost secrets which accompanied her everywhere and which none of us dared to open. And I remembered the tens of thousands of other handbags that I have seen since – bulky, leather receptacles, carrying the junk, or perhaps the gems – of a lifetime. Smart, shiny little purses, geared to an age of plastic money and leaf-thin electronics, worn out relics in imitation of dead fashions and dying trends. And saddest of all, the dusty handbags of the lonely spinster or the forgotten aunt packed away in boxes and finally opened by the hands of strangers who came to bury them. I knew now what Annie's daughter meant. What secrets would she find when she opened that handbag? Would she find a stranger, or would she find the mother she had known and loved for sixty years?

She opened the corner cupboard and brought out the handbag – faded black leather, well worn at the edges – with a short carrying strap and an artificial buckle that snapped it open and shut. As she reverently opened the bag it seemed to contain nothing but papers of every description, receipts for every imaginable service from decades past – electricity, oil, coal, rates, telephone, television licence, letters from her sister in America, prayers and novenas and an overpowering collection of memorial cards, reminders to pray for everyone she had ever known, and a faded birth certificate. Underneath it all was an expensive looking envelope inscribed 'Marriage Certificate' and a couple of out-of-date lottery tickets and, looking like a long lost ancient manuscript a flimsy sheet of paper with the handwritten words of 'The Mountainy Farmer', a well-known local ballad. Buried at the bottom were her rosary beads, worn out with use and repaired with wire and darning thread. Alongside them was a small bottle of perfume, 'Evening in Paris', and a powder puff, as it was called in those days, the only concession to vanity permitted to respectable ladies.

It was all very normal and acceptable. There was nothing to disturb in any way the precious memory Annie's daughter had of her mother. In death as in life, she was still the same gentle parent she had known and loved for sixty years.

Unsung Heroes

We have no hesitation about bestowing honours on those who go into battle on our behalf. We have more of a problem about rewarding those who confront less violent but more emotionally stressful situations on our behalf, and that is a bit unfair, because heroism is not confined to the battlefield. The experts tell us that we begin life with a certain ration of courage, and every time we face the enemy we use up a little of this precious gift, until the day arrives when we throw our hat at ideals of heroism and sacrifice and run for cover as fast as we can. Even the toughest sergeant major will eventually break.

The soldier, however, has one great advantage. He can fight back. He can inflict pain on his opponents and no one will raise an eyebrow in disapproval.

But what about the rest of us? Take for example teachers. They start the school year with their meagre ration of courage, and they confront the enemy, so to speak, five days a week, forty weeks a year, all the while deprived of the right to respond in the same way as the rest of us do in times of crisis – fight or flight. They can neither fight back against their juvenile attackers nor can they run for cover and leave them to fend for themselves. They are expected to stand their ground and endure abuse, lies, noise, fear, stress and sometimes violence while striving to instil some elements of virtue and goodness into their juvenile charges. Such courage in the face of the enemy definitely deserves recognition.

Our present culture is based on a fallacy – that there is no original sin. And before you dismiss that as theological camouflage, consider what it means. Original sin is the belief that, left to ourselves, we will always take the selfish option. Every young child is a living example. A child's attention is entirely focused upon itself. It has no awareness of the needs or the rights of others. If a child sees something that it likes it will reach out and take it, even if another child is holding it. Only when it has been taught that there is a difference between 'mine' and 'yours' will a child begin to practice what we call Christian virtue.

We have to learn generosity and compassion and forgiveness and all the other forms of Christian behaviour, and so must our children. Thinking that we will naturally become kind and loving adults if left to our own devices is a mistake of gigantic proportions.

Film-Making in Days of Yore

In 1963 two Derrymen, John Hume and Terry McDonald, made a half-hour film in black and white called *A City Solitary*. In spite of the limitations of their equipment, the film was so good that it was subsequently shown on Teilifís Éireann and BBC One – where I first saw it.

I had very little experience of movie work at this time, but I thought it should be possible to portray a parish on film in the same way as they had portrayed a city. I took the idea to Terry McDonald and asked would there by any difficulties?

'Yes,' he said, 'Money.'

Equipment could be borrowed, converted or even manufactured, but film stock and processing could only be had for ready cash.

I cannot remember how I got this money, or where, but eventually I bought film – (Plus-X and Tri-X) – and started shooting, using the equipment and experience from *A City Solitary*; and I might mention here that I have been making free use of Terry McDonald's equipment and experience ever since.

Right from the start we broke all the rules – and paid dearly for it. We had no script – it was written when the film was finally edited – and very often no idea of what we wanted. Finally we settled on the theme of the buildings on which most parish activities are focused – the school, the church and the hall. Hence the title *Parish Centre*.

There were endless practical difficulties – problems of lighting large areas, matching slow to fast film, getting sound recordings of a reasonable standard, bringing artists together at a suitable time for filming. One of my most vivid memories is of asking an already weary dance-band to play a tune through 'just once more' – at three o'clock in the morning.

The film was an enormous success locally. The hall was packed on opening night and there were almost as many patrons outside as inside, some of them literally kicking the door to get in.

We sent a copy to Teilifís Éireann some time later and were rather flattered when it was eventually shown on the Horizon programme.

The success of *Parish Centre* was misleading – as I discovered when I was asked to make an hour-long film about the parish of Ballinascreen in Co. Derry. The difficulties of film-making, I quickly learned, increase with the length of the film, according to some kind of geometric progression. The history of this film, beginning with Terry McDonald's escape from drowning in a Holy Lake, and finishing with his claim that a Ballinascreen cow ate his light-meter, would take too long to recount, but these are some of the snags we ran into: we didn't know the district well enough; we had to travel eighty miles for every filming session; we tried to include everything – seven schools, two factories and three churches; we had to wait for reasonably good weather to film in colour.

The people of Ballinascreen were extremely helpful even when it meant working into the small hours of the morning, and their hospitality took a lot of the sting out of the work, but it was a long hard haul – taking two years in all – before we finally had a film ready for showing.

Even then we were not clear of trouble. The publicity campaign fell through completely, due to a newspaper strike, and we found ourselves relying entirely on the merits of the film and word-of-mouth advertising to sell it to the public. Neither was really successful. The sheer labour of Ballinascreen tempered my enthusiasm for film-making for about two years. I did a little work on a film about another parish, but I was not very deeply involved.

Last year, however – I had moved parish in the meantime – I thought I would try another half-hour film, this time for purely local consumption. I used kodachrome reversal film and a separate soundtrack, which meant only one copy of the film, but a big reduction in cost. I concentrated on entertainment rather than education. I introduced a few simple photographic tricks such as fast motion and doubt exposure and they helped the film considerably. However, it wasn't without its disasters. For instance we interviewed a ninety-two-year-old man with the lens cap on – and didn't get back in time for a repeat.

The film was titled *In Sight of Sawel*.

Though the cheapest and quickest film I have made, it was the most enjoyable. There must be a moral there somewhere!

It isn't possible to say what a film costs – either before or after shooting. You can calculate how much you have spent on film stock and processing, but these are only the bones of the film. You must then allow for equipment – if only for wear and tear – for recording tape and magnetic film, for bulbs and lighting equipment, for copyright fees if you are using music background, for travelling expenses, and then keep something in reserve for the unexpected.

There are several other variable factors which will influence the final cost – the quality of the film that is aimed at, the type of film that is used, the type of sound recording system, and fees that may have to be paid to professionals such as musicians or narrators. As an example of the variations that are possible 'Ballinascreen' lasted one hour and five minutes and cost £500. Two years ago in Cork I met a man who had a black and white cutting print of a film lasting one hour and fifteen minutes and up to then he had spent £18,000.

It is, however, possible to make a film for twice the cost of the film stock in your final print. In other words a half-hour film in Kodachrome (1200 feet) can be made for the price of 2400 feet of film – approximately £102. It can be done – but I wouldn't recommend it, for there is absolutely no room for mistakes; and mistakes seem to be built into the film-making process.

Why did I make these films? The honest answer is that I like making films. It would be very comforting if I could claim that these films have revolutionised parish life, but they haven't – at least not that I've noticed. All I can say is that they seem to speak to people where sermons and books fail. Film is the new language of country people, especially since the coming of television. They follow the message of a film, whereas a book containing the same message would have no effect whatever on them. If someone could translate the message of Christ into local visual language then I think the real value of film would be seen, but this would require a unique combination of sanctity and technology.

At one time I had hopes of using film to unify the different districts of any parish, but it hasn't been very successful, principally because it often means attempting the impossible – showing the unity of something that is not a unity. It is much more successful at getting a message to people about their own locality. New techniques of teaching in their own school can be put across very effectively to parents, and Mass in their own church takes on a completely new dimension. It is, of course, ideal for recording important parochial events – and it is surprising how much historical interest these will have after a few years.

There are immense difficulties in the way of using film on a parochial level. Photographic equipment is very expensive and film-making is tedious and time-consuming work. Research, script-writing, planning, filming, editing, and dubbing are only some of the steps involved, and every one of them calls for hard slogging. Editing, for instance, without an editor, is the short way to a nervous breakdown.

To be really effective each aspect of parish life would need to be treated separately and carefully, and this means plenty of time and money. They are scarce commodities in most parishes, but I suppose if anyone is really interested in it he will make the time and raise the money, somehow.

Occasions

Faughanvale Bicentenary

Let me begin with a story about the late James McCafferty. Many of you will no doubt remember him as a very talented musician who accompanied the performers in concerts all over the diocese. On this occasion he was accompanying the turns, as they call them, at a local concert in a country parish hall, and all was going well until the interval when one of the performers, a bagpiper, came to him and explained that he had a problem. He had always been used to playing on the march, so that he found it impossible to begin playing from a standing start. James suggested that a solution might be found if he were to go outside into the car park and march up and down playing his bagpipes, and when the time came for him to perform they would signal to him and he could walk on to the stage playing his bagpipes, which is exactly what he did. There was only one discordant note. As the bagpiper marched on to the stage playing his bagpipes he was seen to be covered in snow.

I mention this story because the very first day I came to Faughanvale Parish I saw a line of people, a line of penitents, as it turned out, standing in the snow outside the sacristy of the old church here. They were waiting for Confessions, and Fr Felix O'Neill, the parish priest at the time always heard confessions in the sacristy so they had to line up outside. Why he did not ask them to line up inside the church and come into the sacristy from that side I have never found out. He was ninety years of age when I went there, still active as parish priest, but not the kind of man from whom one could hope to get reasonably rational and convincing explanations for everything that he did.

In fact, he vigorously opposed any attempt to replace old churches – even at the risk of the parishioners' lives. On one occasion he was told that the front gallery of Mullabuoy Church was dangerous. His defence of the Church was unique and highly risky. After Sunday Mass he ordered the women and children to leave and the men to assemble in the front gallery. Then he said, 'When I say "jump" I want you all to jump up and down.' And they did so – and proved to his satisfaction that the gallery was sound. Whether he had contingency plans if it failed has not been recorded.

The original church here was fairly old and run down even in 1962, and there is a danger that we might assume that this in fact was the church which was built two hundred years ago and has survived down to our own time. In reality, the churches that were built at the end of the eighteenth century were very simple and spartan affairs. More than likely this church was simply a rectangular building, four walls and a roof, with an earthen floor. There would have been no galleries, no seats, no flooring, and very little in the line of furniture or decoration. In fact, a church in Derry was used for the first time for the funeral of the parish priest who had built it, Fr John Lynch. It was unfinished at that stage, so the preacher stood on a pile of builder's rubble that was lying in one corner. Similarly this church in Faughanvale would not have been finished or completed in one operation. More than likely the original church, as I say, consisted of four walls and a roof and an earthen floor. It was only well into the nineteenth century that luxuries, you might say, such as a wooden floor and, even more so, wooden seating, were introduced into the churches of that time.

The spiritual life of the church centred around the Mass and the sacraments in the early part of the nineteenth century. Emphasis would have been laid on baptism and Sunday Mass attendance. Only later did frequent Confession and Holy Communion develop, but near the end of the century or indeed from the middle of the century onwards there was a huge increase in devotions of one kind or another, not merely in saying the rosary but in all kinds of novenas and devotions to particular saints. Parish missions became very popular in the later part of the nineteenth century and through these missions many of the continental devotions and novenas were promoted very strongly. Great devotion to the Pope was preached also by these men, especially after the declaration of Papal Infallibility, and indeed one reads history books today which lament the steady decline of the peculiarly Irish kind of spirituality that was not exactly blotted out but was certainly over-shadowed by the Roman style of Christianity that was brought to Ireland, by clergy who had been educated on the continent.

From the late part of the nineteenth century until the middle of the twentieth century it would be fair to say that very little changed in the Catholic Church in Ireland. While the world went through two world wars, Ireland remained basically unaffected both in its attitudes and its relationship with the outside world, so that the high standard of morality which was part of daily life, and the dreaded fear of sins against morality, was as strong, if not stronger, in 1962 when I came to Faughanvale than it was a hundred years previously. Indeed, Fr Felix O'Neill, the parish priest in 1962 might very well have stepped out of the pages of Canon Sheehan who was writing about Irish clergy a hundred years previously.

Fr O'Neill was rather unique in that he was at that time the only surviving parish priest who had not been appointed by Bishop Farren, and as some of you no doubt remember, Bishop Farren was a fairly authoritarian and somewhat abrasive type of bishop. He did not like to be contradicted, and believed that his priests and his people should display the virtue of obedience at all times to a high degree. Unfortunately, he ran into a problem with Fr O'Neill, who was essentially his own man; and he did not take orders lightly from anyone, so that when it came to a conflict between Bishop Farren's ideas and Fr O'Neill's ideas about what should or should not be done, it usually ended up with Fr O'Neill reminding him in a very patronising voice, 'You're a young man yet, and you have a lot to learn.' The effect of this on Bishop Farren was to turn him almost purple, and he would very aggressively remind Fr O'Neill of his duty to do what his bishop told him, so Fr O'Neill simply patted him on the head and said, 'Jesus meek and humble of heart.' And as you might imagine, to that there is no answer.

Unfortunately, he adopted the same approach to his curates and to his parishioners. Having observed the penitents waiting in the snow for Confession, I decided that one of the first priorities was to install a confession box inside the church, so I got a local man to build a confession box, and one Sunday morning Fr O'Neill arrived down to say Mass and discovered the confession box installed and in action, and he didn't take kindly to this innovation. He didn't say anything at the time but later in the day on Sunday afternoon when I was sitting in my upstairs room watching *Z-Cars* on my black and white television, he landed in and began very aggressively, 'Who told you to put the confession box into the church?' And I said, 'Now if you want to sit down and talk about it we will, but if you're coming up to fight with me I'm not saying a thing.' And he said, 'Who told you to put in this confession box?' So I simply disregarded him completely and continued to watch *Z-Cars*. He continued asking this question for a while and when that didn't work he suddenly whipped out his rosary beads, dropped on his knees beside me and said 'We will pray that God will forgive this curate for his disobedience and that he will learn to obey his parish priest and do what he's told'. And he launched into the rosary. He got, I think, through one decade before he gave up; the competition from *Z-Cars* was a bit too much for him. But the confession box stayed, and the difference of opinion was eventually forgotten.

In my early days in Faughanvale I was told that on the first Sunday of Fr O'Neill's tenure as parish priest – this was in 1937 – he began the twelve o'clock Mass at twenty past twelve, which caught all the regular Mass goers on the hop because they had been accustomed to Fr McEldowney, his predecessor's, more relaxed ways, and one old man was heard to say as he hurried into the chapel, 'God be with good ould Fr McEldowney, barring you came on a Monday morning, you couldn't be late for Sunday Mass.' In my time I tried to persuade Fr O'Neill that starting at twenty past the hour was an injustice to those who came in time for Mass but he always insisted that the people from the hills, as he described them, should be given a little bit of leeway.

Fr O'Neill greatly enjoyed the pastoral side of his priesthood. He wasn't so happy about the managerial and the technical side of it. He found great difficulty in accommodating himself to all the rules and regulations but he thoroughly enjoyed meeting people and talking to them and listening to their stories and telling his stories. The country Stations were a great favourite of his. In those days the Station Mass was held in the morning but that did not mean that Fr O'Neill came home from the Station in the morning. He very often spent the entire day in the Station house. Similarly, doing his sick round, he could be very unpredictable. If the conversation and the company were sufficiently congenial he could sit down and spend a whole afternoon with one patient and forget entirely about all the others who were waiting for him.

Of course this meant that at times like Confirmation he could be most difficult to manage. Everyone was on their best behaviour and tried to avoid anything that might irritate or annoy Bishop Farren. This, however, did not extend to Fr O'Neill. At that time it was customary for the bishop to interview each priest of the parish individually, and the priest would be expected to produce his registers, his visitation books, his Mass books, and so on for examination and very slight mistakes or adjustments could irritate Bishop Farren very quickly so all kinds of efforts were made to make sure that all was to hand for him and that everything was to his liking. So a special room was set aside for this interview. It was usually a bedroom and it would be papered and painted for the occasion and new furniture put into it and a sparkling smooth eiderdown over the bed; everything absolutely clean and shining; and no one was allowed to enter that room until the Bishop had concluded his interviews.

On one occasion, however, after the Confirmations in the church Fr O'Neill went missing and no one could find him high or low. We searched the house, we searched the sheds, we even went back to the church to see if he was there but no one could find him, until eventually it approached the time for the Bishop's examination of the registers and someone checked in this special bedroom to make sure that all was well and there was Fr O'Neill in the bed with his clothes and his boots on, covered with the new eiderdown, fast asleep, not a worry in the world, and I am quite sure hoping that he had really done something worthwhile to annoy Bishop Farren.

Priests came and went to Faughanvale during Fr O'Neill's time in office, all bringing their own brand of faith and humanity and incompetence to the parish. There have been fourteen curates in the parish since I left in 1964 and seven of those are dead. There have been four parish priests and – as might be expected – three of those are dead. One of them in particular, Mgr Ben Kielt, left his mark on the parish, with an immense building programme including the church which has served the parish well to the present day. All are remembered, in their different ways, but Fr O'Neill seems to have left the strongest legacy.

My last memory of him was Christmas morning, 1963. He always brought a bottle of something to 'treat' the collectors. Mostly they were modest men who wouldn't be seen dead with a drink in their hands at eleven o'clock in the morning, but he insisted that they join him, and produced the bottle of Bushmills from his jacket. He soon discovered, however, that there were no glasses and I saw a look of relief passing over the face of the counters as I left. I should have known better. When I returned to the sacristy a couple of minutes later Fr O'Neill and the counters were toasting one another from a selection of large and not too clean flower vases.

A month later he was dead, still in harness at ninety years of age.

Working with him could be a nerve-racking business, but only if you expected him to abide by the rules and regulations that were a normal part of clerical life elsewhere. He was a maverick. He was his own man, and that is no bad thing, for I think every diocese needs a few mavericks. It needs a few men who have no fear of speaking out, who are untouchable in the same way that Fr O'Neill was untouchable. There really wasn't any punishment that a bishop could impose on him that would have had any effect or that would not have appeared to be a gross injustice by being imposed on a man of his years. But his independence of mind helped to keep him open to views and to attitudes that were not popular at the time but which were to prove much more acceptable as the years passed. I recall especially his dismissal of the idea of limbo at a time when limbo was being taught in every Catholic school in the country. This doctrine which distressed so deeply parents whose children had died before Baptism was rejected out of hand, for he instinctively knew that God put people first. 'Limbo is a load of nonsense,' he said. 'The faith of the mother is more than enough to save the child.' And I thought 'what a lovely idea' and I still think it's a lovely idea.

He wrote one article that was published about Our Lady in the 1920s, and in 1963 he was still showing it around with pride, not just because he had published something but because he might have added a new idea or a new point of view to devotion to Our Lady.

Other men have left a legacy of stone and timber, for which they are deservedly remembered. His memory lives on in the hearts of all who knew him.

Killyclogher Reopening

It is customary on occasions such as this to invite a native-born son of the parish who has risen to some degree of eminence in his chosen way of life, and who has displayed an unflinching loyalty and commitment to his native parish down the years, to say a few words. In view, then, of the intense level of scrutiny to which most aspects of life are subjected today, it would be a wise and diplomatic precaution if I were to confess before I go any further that I am here under false pretences, on all three counts.

I am not, in fact, a native-born son of Cappagh Parish. I missed that privilege by a mere four weeks, which is the age at which I migrated from Castlederg to take up residence in Coneywarren. Neither have I risen to any degree of eminence in my chosen way of life, as any of my clerical colleagues will cheerfully testify, and neither have I shown any great degree of loyalty to the parish of Cappagh, because the house in which I was reared lies just inside the parish boundary but it is also three to four miles from both Knockmoyle and Killyclogher churches, and a mere mile from the Sacred Heart Church in Omagh. So for Saturday Confession, Sunday Masses, parish missions and First Communions, and for all other religious ceremonies, instead of supporting Cappagh, you could say I joined the opposition.

I was, though, confirmed in Killyclogher, an occasion of which I have no memory whatever, but I do have a photograph of myself and my sister on Confirmation Day. She had risen from her sick bed to be there, and in the photo she looks rather like a victim of famine, and standing alongside her is myself, looking like I had caused the famine. I was not merely fat: I was wearing short trousers, the ultimate indignity for a ten-year-old. In fact, the only occasion which competes with it for embarrassment was the Silver Jubilee of my Priesthood when I foolishly boasted to the young lady who was serving Mass for me that I could still fit into the soutane which I had worn on the day of my ordination, twenty-five years previously. She looked at me with that air of devious innocence that children wear so well and said, 'Why? Were you always fat?'

In view of all this unfamiliarity with Killyclogher Church I thought it only wise to ask your esteemed parish priest for some historical background on the church and he sent me an article which I duly read, but which talked of purlins and chancels and vaulted ceilings but never mentioned history, the reason for which became clear when I got to the end of the article and found the signature of the architect for this project who, as it happens, lives down the street from me in Limavady, and probably knows as little about the history of Killyclogher as myself. Nonetheless I was able to unearth a few exotic titbits about the parish. For example, even six hundred years ago the people of Cappagh knew that it pays to be nice to bishops. When Archbishop Colton was making his famous inspection of the Derry Diocese in the fourteenth century his first stop was Cappagh, where he was welcomed by the people of the parish and given a whole ox to feed himself and his retinue, before being pointed in the direction of Ardstraw and told that he might find many more things in need of inspection there than he would find in Cappagh, and if that was not enough there was always Derry, some miles further on.

A little less enlightened was the decision four hundred years later to send their parish priest to take part in the notorious Derry Discussion, a week long debate between Catholic and Protestant clergymen from which both sides emerged convinced they had been victorious and more entrenched than ever in their ignorance. On the home front things were a little more encouraging. Early in the eighteen-hundreds the Blessington–Mountjoy Estate gave the site for a church at Knockmoyle, and sometime later a church was built there by the parish priest Daniel O'Flagherty and also a small church at Killyclogher, but it was in 1840 that a protestant landowner called Hope or Homer Wilson gave land to the parish so that it could build a larger church and have space for a graveyard in Killyclogher. It would also seem that the church was largely rebuilt in the 1870s. After that the historical record runs dry. It is the 1920s before the church is mentioned again, this time to record the installation of a new marble altar and two side altars. Everything after that is within living memory.

However, leaving aside the historical record for a moment let us concentrate on the spiritual aspect of parish life here in Killyclogher. One of the most favoured quotations from scripture for occasions like this is the line from chapter three of Exodus: 'The place in which you stand is holy ground.' If you read newspaper accounts of church openings a hundred years ago the chances are that they will begin with these words. And they are appropriate words because this is indeed a holy place, but not holy because it is a building dedicated to the worship of God, nor because it is shaped and constructed in a way that makes its religious purpose immediately recognisable, nor because holy functions and services are celebrated here, but because generation after generation of people from this community have sat or stood or knelt before God in this church and offered him an unending chorus of worship as an expression of their relationship with God.

We find worship a difficult concept to grasp nowadays, so much of our culture is concentrated on ourselves – self-sufficiency, self-indulgence, self-possessed, self-supporting, self-service, even self-harm – while worship is directed away from self, towards God. Worship is the time we give to God alone. How we spend that time is not that important. Merely to stand silently before God is to worship God, but for us Catholics the ultimate worship is to offer the sacrifice of Christ to God His Father – in short, to offer Mass. I continually bore my congregation with the statement that if you believe in God you must worship God. If you do not worship God your belief is false. When young people tell me that they belong to the Catholic Church but they don't go to Mass I tell them I belong to the Manchester United Football team but I don't play football. One statement is as sensible as the other.

This is a holy place, because the people have made it holy. Down the years and the generations they have come here faithfully every Sunday to worship God, and they have passed that belief on to their children and their children's children, and as long as they continue this practice this will remain a holy place, and for that reason this church is a place they can be proud of.

However, lest someone say, 'Have the clergy played no part in this story?' let me reply by recalling just a few of the priests who have struggled, in their own limited way, to maintain the holiness of life of this particular parish.

My earliest memory is of Fr John McKenna, a gentle soul, universally known to the clergy as 'Black John', not for any uncomplimentary reason but because of the colour of his hair and to distinguish him from his classmate, also Fr John McKenna, who inevitably was known as 'White John'. When I first knew Fr Black John McKenna he was neither white nor black. At that time 'shining' might have been a more appropriate title. He died while hearing confessions, not as has been suggested, because he was submerged beneath the heavy tide of sinfulness that he encountered in Killyclogher, but rather because he was such a compassionate confessor that customers came from far and near and dramatically increased the odds that he would die in the confessional.

His successor, Fr Chapman, vainly tried to interest the parishioners of Cappagh in a little musical culture. He was a proficient violinist, with what one might call an artistic temperament, who finally hung up his fiddle and bow, having signally failed to interest a Killyclogher audience in the delights of Bach's *Air* on a G-string.

Fr Willie Dolan tried to pass on to us younger clergy his interest in art and antiques, pointing out to us that the real Waterford Crystal was not the shiny stuff that we paid exorbitant prices for in the local gift shops, but the dull uninspiring examples from the nineteenth century which adorned his shelves. He acquired an impressive collection of oil paintings – at what we now know were ridiculously low prices – and derived a great pleasure simply from viewing them. When age and infirmity began to overtake him, he sold off the entire collection by auction, gave away the proceeds to different causes and retired to Nazareth House in Bishop Street in Derry, a mere hundred metres from the house where his successor Fr Francis Murray was reared.

Fr Murray might seem a most unlikely drill sergeant in his present guise, but during his time in Limavady, where he was curate for many years, his altar servers could do a synchronised right turn with a precision that would have been the envy of the Brigade of Guards. Nothing to compare with it had ever been seen in Limavady up to that time and sadly nothing to compare with it has been seen in Limavady ever since. Since moving to Cappagh Fr Murray's expertise has branched out in numerous directions, particularly in the field of finance, which must be a great source of comfort to his successor Fr Boland, who, I am sure, fully intends to punch a large hole in Fr Murray's nest egg.

Today we celebrate the reopening of this church of Killyclogher and we rightly rejoice in the beauty of its restoration, but what of tomorrow? What future lies in store for the people of this parish? Let's not underestimate the problem. The Church in Ireland is in dire straits at the moment, and the clergy have accelerated its downward slide. As one gets older one tends to disregard the trivia and the diversions of life and to focus on the essentials, and the one essential for us is the sacrifice of Christ on the Cross, the sacrifice which was anticipated at the Last Supper and that is recalled and re-enacted every day in the Mass.

Go to Mass every Sunday, and bring your children to Mass every Sunday and do not ask them would they like to go to Mass any more than you would ask them would they like to do their homework. The Mass is work, religious work. It takes effort and concentration, so don't try to sell it as entertainment. This is the only wisdom I have to offer you. If you go to Mass every Sunday; if you take your children to Mass every Sunday, then this church will continue to be a holy place and you will be a holy people.

Joint Opening,
St Mary's Limavady

When I was growing up in the forties and fifties on the outskirts of Omagh we had a distant neighbour called Andy John Porter, a sort of farmer plus occasional cattle dealer. He caught our attention as children because his physical size was in direct contrast to his knowledge of the modern world, which was positively microscopic. When Eddie Montague opened a cinema in Dromore, Andy John attended the first show, a rollicking pirate yarn full of gratuitous violence and much swinging from ropes and general smashing up of the furniture. As he left the cinema Andy John is reported to have asked a companion, 'I wonder where Montague keeps all them wild men at night?'

He was equally at sea with television. I spent most of an hour on one occasion trying to persuade him that the horse race he was watching on the screen was actually happening in England at the same time. Nonetheless, he was a down to earth, successful businessman and a frequent visitor to our house in his overburdened little Austin a30, which he brought to a halt by the simple expedient of lifting his foot from the accelerator and letting the laws of mechanics do the rest. He was also a solid churchgoing Presbyterian and sometimes his visit coincided with evening prayer in our house, which consisted of the rosary followed by an endless litany of prayers for all sorts of intentions, but Andy John simply sat down with us and silently prayed his own prayers for his own intentions until we had finished.

We didn't discuss religious beliefs – you had to be a personal friend of someone before you could discuss doctrine honestly, and if for some reason or other it cropped up unexpectedly you usually sidestepped it in the fashion of Sammy Fleck, another good Presbyterian, this time from Larne, who was asked by a mischievous Catholic if he believed in Purgatory. Sammy thought for a while and then said, 'I don't know about Purgatory but I hope there is a hell for there's a few boys around here I'd like to see in it.'

I learned about church unity from Andy John and men like him. They knew instinctively that it was more important to love your neighbour than to understand him. We don't pretend to know the intricacies of other people's path to God. Indeed we have trouble finding our own way to heaven. We just want to share with others our belief that the way to salvation is never easy and that we need to help one another along the path to eternal life – a path that is sometimes stony on the feet and hard to follow. And that is why the reopening of this church would be so much less meaningful if it were not shared by so many of our neighbours.

If we can avoid misleading one another then I think we will be doing very well. I recall reading about Hitler's Big Lie theory in my youth which suggested that if you want to convince people you should tell not a small lie but a big lie because the big lie is easier to believe. Since the renovation of this church began I've had parishioner after parishioner say to me that the sand blasting did a great job on those stones, when in fact not a single stone on this church has been sandblasted. The pointing was drilled out and replaced and the stones later washed down with an ordinary hosepipe but somehow sandblasting has evidently caught the public imagination so from now onwards the legend will probably be printed instead of the truth.

It's not that the sandblasting story is going to do any great harm – unless, of course, some innocent clergyman hears of it and thinks that he can improve the look of his church by blasting all before him – but there is a danger that other fables and other legends will be given equal credence. A man said to me recently: 'This renovation will be a great memorial to you when you're gone.' (He didn't say 'dead and gone' but I think that's what he meant.) Now that kind of lie really worries me. To talk about memorials and monuments is a bit like the man who was recommended for some parish job and his promoter said that he would be 'an ornament to the parish' but a more cynical member of the congregation was heard to say, 'Aye, he'll be like most ornaments, expensive and useless.'

There's only one reason for renovating a church, and that is because it needs to be done. If you want memorials, go to a graveyard. Don't ever imagine you will be remembered for some building repair you have done. If you want to be remembered, if you really want people to talk about you, do nothing. Let the buildings fall into ruin and decay, and I guarantee they'll never *stop* talking about you.

Anyway, I'm pleased it all turned out so well. Getting it right is such a chancy thing. We look at the plans and think 'Yes, that will work' but as it begins to take shape you start worrying. Even picking colours is fraught with danger. I am a great magnolia man myself for interior decorating – it's a fairly safe choice for philistines like myself – but you have to venture out from the shore. You have to trust the judgement of others with more training and experience, and besides, you can always blame them if it turns out to be a disaster.

However, to my jaundiced eye, it has all turned out quite well. Put it this way, as I have said already this week, if I were doing it over again I would still employ the same team. They believe in getting things as right as possible.

However, when all has been renewed and repaired this is still a place of worship, and if people do not worship here we have wasted our time and our money. As I have said so often, if we believe in God, we must worship God. If we do not worship God, our belief is false. The ultimate reason for our work is to draw people together to worship God. 'Unless the Lord build the house, they labour in vain who build it.'

Corradina Mass Rock

The town of Limavady where I presently labour is perhaps better known to the outside world for its ecumenical encounters of twenty years ago, when a local Presbyterian minister was forced into retirement for participating in some ecumenical gestures with his Catholic colleague just across the road. He should, perhaps, have known better, and been better prepared for trouble. The very street names which distinguish the town are not the boringly ubiquitous High Street and Main Street and Bridge Street that you find in other towns, but instead the citizens have asserted their origins and their identity with names like Protestant Street and Plantation Road, Bishop's Road and Irish Green Street, Church Street and Scotchtown Road. Indeed, we take a quiet pride in preserving our differences so we point out with some smugness for the benefit of the occasional visitor one of the few stained-glass windows that I know of in Northern Ireland showing Mass being celebrated in Penal days. You can see it in St Mary's Church in Irish Green Street, first on the left as you approach the altar. Like the picture itself the title is somewhat melodramatic. 'A Christmas Mass in the Penal Days' with the ominous subtitle 'The Alarm'. It is a poorly executed version of a painting that has hung in thousands of Irish houses over the years, depicting the same scene and giving a dubious credibility to the many myths and legends that have buttressed the lives of the ordinary Catholic for generations, but probably have little or nothing to do with historical accuracy.

A fully vested priest says Mass in the snow. His vestments are clean and ironed, the missal is the size of a building block. In the distance we can see two lookouts – or maybe more serious supporters, for they are both carrying guns – and the lookouts are shouting a warning as the Red Coats dash up the valley with fixed bayonets. The components of Cromwellian persecution combined with nineteenth-century Fenianism and supplemented by the basic legends of the Penal days make this an iconic image of the struggle for religious freedom. Historical accuracy is not the criterion. It is much more important to preserve the legend of Catholic persecution.

In fact, clergy generally were not at risk of their lives during Penal times. Bishops and members of religious orders were expelled from the country but most of the diocesan clergy continued in their parishes, though under tough and oppressive circumstances. They had to register their names and locations with the authorities but they could say Mass in what where called Mass houses (but in reality were little more than lean-tos against the gable wall). The persecution – or the lack of it – depended greatly on the attitude of the local landlord. He could turn a blind eye to a lot, but he could also be a puritanical fanatic bent on destroying the catholic faith. But destruction of the faith was a rare ambition. The Penal Laws were directed against the property of Catholics, especially Catholic land, and by the end of the eighteenth century Catholic ownership of land had gone from more than half to a mere five per cent. The professions were closed to Catholics. They couldn't be soldiers, sailors, lawyers or civil servants. They couldn't buy land and they couldn't pass it on to their eldest sons. It had to be divided among all the sons in the family. The only way to get around these restrictions was to take the Oath of Loyalty to the Crown which involved, among other things, denying transubstantiation and receiving Communion according to the Rite of the Church of Ireland.

In spite of all this the ordinary people displayed an amazingly persistent loyalty to their faith. There were countless good reasons for giving way – if your children were hungry you didn't worry too much about theological definitions – but it was not because they understood their faith or were intellectually convinced by its doctrines that they hung on. In fact, they had some really appalling ideas about the Trinity and the Incarnation and the whole plan of salvation, but they had a firm habit of faith, what we would call a virtue, whereby they put the Mass at the centre of their lives as their parents had done before them and as they hoped their children would do after them. They did not need to think about it. It just felt right and they kept on doing it, and when they looked back years later they knew in their hearts that they had done the right thing.

The belief that the Penal days were dedicated unswervingly to the extermination of priests and bishops is too simple. Certainly many priests paid with their lives but it was because they were seen as politically dangerous rather than spiritually misleading. Bishops could influence the minds of their flock. Jesuits and Franciscans had been trained in the Papal universities and seminaries of the continent and were full of dangerous and subversive ideas. The diocesan clergy on the other hand were no threat. They were poorly educated. They hadn't travelled far, and were mostly looking for a quiet parish to live out their days in peace and safety. They didn't present any great danger to the Crown. Indeed, if we take a practical example from the end of the eighteenth century, we can see how things really were. In my former parish of Longtower in Derry City the parish priest began building a church in 1786. The biggest donation by far came from the Church of Ireland Bishop and the next biggest came from the Protestant Corporation. Of course there were exceptions to the rule and some paid a high price for their allegiance to the catholic faith. Nonetheless, there are two lessons I would like you to take home with you. Firstly, the loyalty of the Irish people to the Mass and the Eucharist was sustained at even the worst of times by the simple practice of going to Mass. That teaching still holds true. No amount of education in the faith will substitute for the regular practice of the faith. As we offer Mass in our community today we relive the experience of offering Mass that was part of our history and part of our growing up. In the 1960s I watched an old lady take a crust from her pocket to sustain her on her journey home from twelve o'clock Mass. She had fasted from twelve o'clock the night before and had walked three miles to the church and was now heading home. Do you think she could ever have lost her faith?

The second lesson is 'the past is past'. We must be reconciled with the enemies of yesterday. Every month I meet with a group of ministers from the other churches. We study the Bible, but mostly we chat and drink tea. It is a marvellous experience of fraternity. If you ever intend having an argument with someone may I suggest that first you sit down and have tea and a chat. We have different approaches to the teaching of Jesus Christ but we learn to close the gap by listening respectfully to one another and careful listening has taught us that everyone has a firm belief in the presence of Jesus Christ. The manner of that presence may differ but the fact of His presence is indisputable. We still have our street names but they are a relic of the past rather than an expression of the present. I am quite happy to walk down Protestant Street and my companions walk sedately down Irish Green Street. At the end of the day the people of the present are more important to us than the places of the past.

Beatification of Edmund Rice

It is good to see so many of you gathered here for this celebration of the Beatification of Edmund Ignatius Rice, the founder of the Irish Christian Brothers. Such occasions are rare – and one might be tempted to say, growing rarer – so it is only right that we should celebrate with joy and with not a little pride.

The Christian Brothers themselves have shown an exemplary degree of forgiveness by not merely inviting their diocesan bishop to preside at this celebration but also by allowing a member of the diocesan clergy to preach at it, for their beloved founder endured much persecution in his day at the hands of both parties. He was described by his own bishop as 'one of our factious lay subjects, a butcher, a public fornicator, who is at the head of the small quarrelsome groups who give trouble to their bishop and to his diocese'. Even worse, he was described by some of the local clergy as 'a cattle dealer' – always a very dubious profession – 'an impertinent intruder in the affairs of the sanctuary' who 'was of irregular habits and of lustful desires, which to the prejudice of public morality and the scandal of the faithful he fully gratified', etc.

It is only fair to point out that the ringleader of these clergy and the unfortunate bishop both came to rather sticky ends. The bishop's own colleagues in the Province of Cashel wrote to Rome in terms that one rarely encounters in polite episcopal circles, recommending that he be suspended from his duties, and he was in fact in Rome shortly afterwards awaiting trial when he died. The priest was shown to have had a much more lurid lifestyle than he had accused Edmund Rice of living and he was forced to retire in disgrace by Rome. In the Annals of the Diocese of Waterford and Lismore, the 1820s were not one of their finest hours.

I mention these events, not to pass judgement on the deplorable state of the Diocese of Waterford in 1820 but to illustrate the completely irrational and unforeseen obstacles that a holy man may have to overcome in order to fulfil his vocation. We sometimes think of the saint as a man removed from the world, his life centred around his prayers and his spiritual exercises, cut off from the busy frenzy of public life and the distraction of business. In fact, the saint is probably, at the end of the day, a better businessman than any of us, because he manages and he organises his affairs successfully without ever losing touch with his primary aim, which is to know God, to love God, and to serve God.

To be a saint of the Church I think three things are necessary. One, you must be lucky; two, you must be sincere; three, you must persevere. If being lucky seems a rather unspiritual virtue, it is, but unless you are lucky no one will know about your holiness – except God. You will be crowned in heaven for your good works, but your name will be forgotten on earth. You must be sincere so that your determination depends on no one's good opinion but your own. And thirdly you must persevere because, as we have seen, the obstacles that you anticipate will be mere molehills in comparison with the obstacles that you will actually encounter.

I'm sure I do not need to recount to this congregation the early life of Edmund Rice. Most will I am sure, be better versed in it than me. Suffice it to say that he was a well-to-do Waterford merchant who sold up his business and with a few companions dedicated himself to the education of poor Catholic boys. If I may digress for a moment; to get some idea of the need for Catholic schools and Catholic education at that time let us jump forward to 1854, fifty years after Edmund Rice started out, to the time when the Brothers came to Derry and set up a school there. On the first day two hundred and ninety boys arrived looking for places. We can only wonder how they were supposed to get an education or where they were supposed to get an education before the Brothers arrived. It must surely have been an even grimmer situation fifty years earlier.

To promote education Edmund Rice had to provide schools and teachers and that meant all the educational bureaucracy that we still have to cope with today. Suitable premises, qualified staff, maintenance of records, maintenance of buildings, loans and overdrafts, fundraising and canvassing, hiring and sometimes firing, persuading and cajoling, explaining and defending, encouraging and restraining, and all the time keeping an eye out for the unexpected, like a maverick bishop or a deranged parish priest. It was hard grinding work, calling for an immense physical and spiritual energy, but before he knew what he had done he had planted a tree that has spread its branches over the entire globe. The very speed at which his schools multiplied, the enthusiasm with which his work was welcomed everywhere, the number of foundations that he saw completed in his own lifetime, all are tangible and irrefutable proofs of the quality of the man and the necessity of his work.

And what of today? How has the vision of Edmund Rice endured after almost two hundred years?

In the developed world the situation has changed radically. Education is no longer the privilege of the few. It is not merely available to all who want it – and even a few who don't want it. It is now an obligatory part of every child's development, leaving a limited demand for the services of the Christian Brothers and other teaching orders. But in the developing world and especially in the poorer countries, the need is still there, and the talents of the Christian Brothers are still in demand. And as in the past, where the need was greatest vocations flourished, and thank God in the poorer countries today that still holds true.

And what is the perception of the Brothers in the minds of today's public? What image do they project to the world? Sadly, some mistaken perceptions have survived from the past, and some new criticisms have put them under the scrutiny of a modern and not always friendly microscope. In a mistaken view of their role and their vocation some people still see the Brothers as second-class clergy, men who for one reason or another have failed to take the final step to ordination and priesthood. No amount of explanation or clarification of their role seems able to dispel this illusion or to convince them that they are Brothers because that is their vocation and they will hopefully remain Brothers to the end of their days.

Present day criticisms are equally difficult to defeat. No one will deny that the discipline of their schools was forceful and occasionally excessive. Physical punishment and military discipline were a part of the culture, but to equate these with physical abuse and on that basis to condemn them is to misunderstand that age entirely, and to judge the achievements of the past by the standards of the present. Of course there were Christian Brothers who instilled fear into their pupils by the use of physical punishment. And there were lay teachers who had an equally firm belief in the benefits of muscular Christianity. And there were even lady teachers from this town, some of them not that tall, who scared the life out of me when I was a child; and come to think of it, some of them still frighten me. But we lived in a violent age. In fact, we lived in the most violent age that the human race has ever known. We were brought up during a war in which fifty million people died violent deaths at the hands of their fellow men. We lived in an age when flogging was still a part of the judicial system. We lived in an age when men and women – sometimes innocent men and women – were hanged by the neck until they were dead. We lived at a time when psychology was in its infancy and where it was an unquestioned principle of education that to spare the rod was to spoil the child. To say that all Christian Brothers were violent men is an unjust and an unsustainable slander. Certainly Br Hamil's Friday tests used to send a shiver of dread down my spine and his methods of punishment on occasion could be classed as unorthodox, to say the least. But Br Burn's habit of bringing a hurley stick into class and whacking balls off the back wall of the classroom was merely an enjoyable diversion, and I can still recall with glee the occasion when he leaned back over the obligatory Sacred Heart lamp for a breather and set his hair on fire. As for Br O'Connell, the nearest he came to violence was one occasion when we were reciting the Litany of Our Lady as always before heading home and the chorus of 'Pray For Us', 'Pray For Us' was getting more and more ragged until we finally halted altogether, but the 'Pray For Us', 'Pray For Us' continued on automatic pilot, memorably led by Frankie Quinn, until Br O'Connell seized his school bag and upended the contents over his head. And in more recent times it has been my privilege to share a house with a Christian Brother for several years and a man less prone to violence I doubt if you will find on the face of this planet.

Discipline is a major issue on today's educational front, even in classes of twenty or so pupils. Discipline in a class of sixty or more pupils in the past was taken for granted. What was expected in addition was a high standard of education. True enough the idea of one-to-one tuition was not unknown in those days, but it worked to a very different and sometimes noisier set of rules. One thing, however, is certain. No ten-year-old ever disrupted a class, much less closed down the entire plant, in a school run by the Christian Brothers.

In his homily in Rome on the occasion of the Beatification of Edmund Rice, Cardinal Daly said that people should not be invited to enter religious life today primarily for motives of service to others. I can only agree with him, but I must also say that it is a pity that no one said this earlier, for the service of others and forgetfulness of self was the high motivation laid before many of us to enter clerical life, and it was not always enough.

Heroic virtue calls for something more than good intentions. It demands a grace that can uplift and inspire when the realities of life begin to press down upon us, as they often do. The reality of a Christian Brother's life was always spartan and sometimes grim – even though the Brothers themselves will be the first to gloss over it – but everything is comparative. If you rise at 5.30 a.m. every week day you appreciate a sleep in until 6.30 a.m. on a Sunday. The physical life was tough but the real sacrifice was the loss of personal freedom. The promise to go where you were sent, do what you were told, live with the company chosen for you and utter no complaint was no easy task. It was and still is a heroic life, and we can only thank God that down the years so many men have been inspired by the example of their founder and have left all in the service of God and neighbour. I do not think I can end in any better way than by quoting the prayer which Edmund Rice composed especially for his newly established institute of religious Brothers:

> Accept, O merciful Jesus, the offering we make of ourselves to Thee: Grant that, all our affections being concentrated in Thee and living for Thee alone, we may be Thine both in life and death, and may pass to that blessed immortality where we shall see Thee face to face and be forever occupied in singing forth Thy praises. Amen.

Centenary,
Sacred Heart Church, Omagh

About six weeks ago I was in the War-on-Want bookshop at the back of Boots, 'screenging' – as my mother would have put it – for a bargain, and I came across a small green-backed volume entitled *A History of the Catholic Church* by John F. O'Doherty. Unlike the other books on the shelves it was not priced and I wondered if there might be a reason for this. Perhaps in this town this book was special, but when I brought it to the girl at the counter she merely looked it over, without recognition and said, 'One pound fifty.'

I had hoped that she might say to me, 'This is a rather special book, because it was written by a man who was once a curate here in Omagh and who was one of the keenest – if not the keenest – minds ever to serve in the Derry Diocese.' And I would have answered, 'Yes, I know. In fact I heard him preach on a Good Friday long ago from that pulpit and I remember to this day exactly what he said.'

He looked down in silence upon us, as preachers did in those days – no politically correct nonsense about talking down to your audience – and then he finally spoke – remember this was three o'clock on a Good Friday. 'Why did Christ have to die on the Cross?' he asked, loudly and deliberately. 'Why did Christ have to die on the Cross?' And again he paused before he spoke. 'He died because he deserved it.' Anyone whose mind was wandering at that point brought it rapidly back into focus. It was not what we were used to hearing on a Good Friday. 'He died because he deserved it.' He went on to explain that if Jesus had taken the guilt of the world upon his shoulders, if he had accepted responsibility for every murder, for every rape, for every betrayal, for every abuse that the human race had perpetrated then he certainly deserved to die. I don't know how the theologians would have assessed his ideas, but he certainly got our attention. If a ten-year-old can remember a sermon for more than fifty years then it had to be fairly good.

That is my memory of the Sacred Heart Church in Omagh – sitting in the ninth or tenth row, listening to the preacher in that magnificent pulpit. At Mass the priest used to take off his chasuble and lay it aside before he climbed into the pulpit. It was like a man laying aside his jacket and rolling up his sleeves as if to say, 'Right, let's get down to business. There's important work to be done!' Of course, there was a steady procession of priests over the years, both in and out of the pulpit, and they all brought their own peculiar talent to the job, some more memorable than others. There was Monsignor McShane – if you live long enough as parish priest of Omagh you generally get to be a monsignor – Monsignor McShane striding down the aisle after Mass and vigorously shaking the free-standing poor-box to estimate the takings from the intensity of the rattle. Fr John Carlin, mouthing and annunciating every word so that the simplest announcement sounded like a royal proclamation. Fr Seamus Shiels, who financed an entire school building programme with his carnivals and dances, and who assured me that he could come home at five in the morning, take a cold shower and a cup of tea and head out for another day's work without even flinching. It doesn't surprise me in the least. Dr Marron who was notorious for his scathing remarks, though I'm disappointed to discover that he was not – as legend had it – changed out of the parish because of his pointedly negative remarks on the course of the war. And of course, the curate – who shall be nameless – who threw me out of that confession box over there. Well, he didn't exactly throw me out. He made me an offer I couldn't refuse. Either I get out or he would come round and throw me out!

There were many others but I don't think any of them quite matched up to the presence and the command of Dr O'Doherty when he was on form, and for that reason I'm slightly disappointed that in Fr Gerry Convery's otherwise magnificent book celebrating the centenary, *Poetry in Stone: Sacred Heart Church, Omagh: A Centenary Appreciation,* there is no individual photograph of John F. O'Doherty. Just a vague figure in the background, and he was much more than this.

Of course, other photographs in this book got my undivided attention – especially the clerical students in their white shirts and black ties from the fifties. They look like apprentice undertakers. Believe it or not, at one time in Omagh there were twenty-five students for the priesthood. They may not all have stayed the course, but by any standards it was an impressive number. As I look around me today at some of the survivors I can only regret that we cannot give them the same kind of renovation and facelift that we have given this church. Their need is so much greater.

The photographs of the clerical students arose out of their involvement in the preparation at that time for the consecration of this church. Fr Seamus Shiels recruited us as pew-polishers and seat-stainers but was wise enough to keep us in the background for the actual ceremony. There was much mysterious coming and going, seats stored in piles while the floors were sprinkled and the walls anointed. There was, however, one major crisis which has never been recorded, but which came to me from an absolutely reliable eyewitness.

Great amounts of holy water were consumed in the course of the ceremony, so much so that when Bishop Farren called out for more holy water there was no holy water to be found. Lesser men would have been found wanting in such a crisis – especially a crisis involving Bishop Farren – but Joe Given, as ever, rose to the occasion. He reached for the nearest bucket, filled it from the nearest tap with water and handed it over to Bishop Farren, having, of course, bowed to the Bishop both before and after the handing over, and the Sacred Heart Church, Omagh, was duly consecrated with Glenhordial Best and has fared none the worse for it down the years.

The photographs in Fr Convery's book also highlight some distinctive features and furnishings of the church and even illustrate some of its more notable possessions. Four sets of cloth-of-gold vestments are modelled by Fr Eugene Hasson, a man for whom dressage is second nature. However, there appears to be a trace of impish humour on the part of the photographer. To add to the solemnity of his pose Fr Hasson is wearing a biretta – the four-cornered hat with the three flanges and a tassel that the priest wore on his way to and from the altar for Mass, and not just any old biretta, but a monsignor's biretta with purple tassel. In the first three photographs, however, the photographer has inexplicably cut off his head at the ears, but in the fourth photograph all is revealed. Fr Eugene is wearing the biretta back to front.

This church has served its purpose impressively over the past hundred years, but how well does it serve the needs of today? The history of church renovation and modernisation in recent years has not been entirely happy. In fact, it resembles nothing so much as the early years of the Reformation in England. The pre-Reformation Church was a rich mixture of devotion to the Mass, belief in the influence of relics and novenas, trust in individual saints to deal with individual problems, countless feasts and fasts and processions, and a rich awareness of everyone's place and hence everyone's responsibilities in the Christian community. There were few educated people, few who had any acquaintance – much less familiarity – with doctrines like transubstantiation or dangers like monophysitism. They believed what they were taught and expressed their approval in their own way. When concelebration was unknown – and that's not going back too many years – the worshippers followed the progress of the different Masses being said around the church and at the 'Sacring' – or what we would call the consecration – they raised their hands to heaven in worship, and then moved on to repeat the performance at the next Mass.

Relics of the saints were to be found everywhere, most of them of very dubious origins, but they didn't alarm the dedicated follower too much. It was the saint in heaven rather than the bones on earth which brought their request before God, and there were saints for all seasons. They varied in popularity with the times and the location, but local saints were a feature of every parish, and every parish was the pride and the property of all its parishioners. They guarded its boundaries jealously – beating the bounds at

Rogationtide was a long-standing annual custom. They listened carefully for their name on the bede-roll, a list of everyone who had made even a small contribution to the well-being of the parish, and they prayed, and encouraged others to pray, for the souls of the dead, for living and dead were all part of the one community.

Then came the Reformation and the attack – subdued under Henry VIII but more intense under Edward – on all the old traditions and practices. The images were removed or painted over, the altars were broken up, the relics were destroyed, the processions were forbidden, the bede-roll was abolished, and prayers for the dead were branded as superstition.

One can imagine the turmoil that all the ordinary people were thrown into as, bit by bit, their entire cultural, social and religious life was overturned and demolished, but the law was the law and no one wanted to finish up on the executioner's block.

Then came the reign of the Catholic Queen Mary and the whole process was put into reverse – but not quite. It would be easy to understand the catholic powers ruthlessly uprooting everything that had gone before, but they were wise enough and honest enough to know that there is no rebellion without cause for rebellion and that much in the medieval church needed updating and reforming. So they reinstated the Mass and the prayers for the dead and the saints and even the relics but they tightened up their standards enormously and retained the most basic and essential reforms of their predecessors, and had Queen Mary lived longer who knows what the outcome would have been – not merely for England but think what a Catholic England would have meant for us.

The liturgical reforms of the past thirty years have followed a similar pattern. In the first phase everything came under attack and many old and distinguished churches were vandalised in the name of reform. Eventually it was realised that reform must be interpreted and applied in accordance with the age and character of the church. The bare walls and empty spaces of a new church may be an essential part of its artistic integrity, whereas the bare walls and empty spaces of an old church may be nothing more than mute evidence of liturgical vandalism. Today, people are more vocal and are prepared to make known their feelings – sometimes quite trenchantly – when the fate of their church is in question.

This church is a happy example of what can be achieved – it is beyond doubt still the church of my childhood and yet there is a sparkle to it, a freshness that commands attention in this age and that proclaims confidence in the times to come. Many ask what is the shape of the church of the future? What part will buildings like the Sacred Heart Church, Omagh, play in the world to come? I wish I knew. The Catholic Church is changing rapidly and the fate of its buildings is anything but secure. But if the ancient Buddhist Temples of China are being reopened by public demand, and gurus of every shape and colour are filling the RDS in Dublin with seekers of peace, and the solemn ceremonies of the Eastern faiths, complete with incense and holy water and gorgeous ceremonial robes, are being shown on national television channels as the way forward, then we, who have practised these things for centuries, must have great hope for the future. We have been sharply reminded that there was much in our Church that needed reformation. Now it is up to us to show the world that there is much in our Church which needs to be treasured.

Obituaries

Frank Devine

The last words I spoke to Frank Devine were strangely ironic. I had called with him to deliver a photograph of himself and Bishop Lagan taken at my Jubilee, and I mentioned that I had to go into hospital for an examination the next day. He was very sympathetic, and wished me all kinds of good luck before I left.

On Wednesday he came to the Penitential Service in Limavady and called around beforehand to see how I had got on. I told him that they had found nothing sinister, and he was delighted for me. We talked about health in general, and how important it was, for I knew he had been in hospital some time earlier, and I finished up by saying, 'It's comforting to know that you are not going to die.' I should have said 'you're not going to die immediately' but, reflecting on it afterwards, and even though I was referring to myself and not to Frank, I couldn't help thinking that it takes talent of a really high order to get things so spectacularly wrong.

If there is one thing that Christ emphasised to his followers it was that death will sneak up on us no matter what anyone may say or do.

> So stay awake because you do not know the day or the hour. … So stay awake because you do not know when the master of the house is coming … if he comes unexpectedly he must not find you asleep. What I say to you, I say to all, Stay Awake. … You know very well that the day of the Lord is going to come like a thief in the night. It is when people are saying 'How quiet and peaceful it is that the worst happens'.

And on and on it goes; the relentless warning that death cannot be predicted. It cannot be second guessed. And that is because it is in God's hands.

We would never make a rash claim to know the mind of God, but we certainly act on occasions as though we did. We plan our lives, far ahead, blithely assuming that our plan will be fulfilled, and only when some unforeseen event brings it crashing to a halt, only then do we begin to suspect that God may not have agreed with our plan.

God does not make bad decisions, He does not make mistakes, so we must delve into the events of Frank's death and see if we can get even a glimpse of what was in the mind of God when he called Frank Devine from this world.

Frank was above everything else, a people person. He loved to meet people and talk to them 'about anything' that interested them. He was always at ease with people, and they always at ease with him. We all know people who send us scurrying for cover when they appear, because they bore the socks off everyone with their conversation, or because they have an inflated idea of their own importance, or because they never know when to go home.

Frank, on the other hand, was the kind of man who was welcomed into any group because he always added to the occasion. There were no pretensions about him. He did not mind whether you were a prince or a pauper. He was always himself. He never tried ot impress you with the intellectual level of his conversation, nor did he try to drop names nor quote influential friends. He was the same to everyone because he was secure in his own personality.

His interest in people lent power to his memory of people. He knew people the length and breadth of the country, and most of the country knew him. His dealing career brought him into personal contact with so many people, but his interest in the dealing business also drew him into that Mafia-like fraternity of dealers who among other things maintain an intelligence branch that would be the envy of any government. The ostensible purpose of the dealers' activity is to make a living, but if you were to offer them a generous pension and then deprive them of the joy of meeting up with one another, of haggling over the price of a drop calf, or of leaning up against the wall of a mart catching up on the latest gossip, there would be no contest.

I can speak with some authority on this matter since I come from dealing stock myself, and I can remember my mother telling me about spending lonely nights in a tenement flat in the Gorbals of Glasgow, listening patiently to my father and his dealing cronies discussing the latest fair they had attended and the latest deal they had struck. It was their only subject of conversation. They consorted with no one other than dealers, and they discussed nothing other than the deals they put together. Whether Frank reached these extremes of involvement or not I cannot say, but dealing was for him a joy as it was for the rest of the fraternity, and to deprive them of it was rather like depriving a drug addict of his fix.

Closely affiliated to Frank's dealing was his smoking. Today's generation regards smoking as a vice, to be stamped out by every means available. My generation and Frank's was encouraged to smoke. It was a social grace, an expression of polite behaviour. Only a mean-spirited individual would fail to offer you a cigarette on first meeting, and at wakes and weddings the respected citizen always kept a generous supply of cigarettes for the guest and the mourner. Smoking was a part of Frank's culture, so that any attempt to deprive him of his liberty or his tobacco would have met with stern resistance. The question had to be asked, 'Is life worth living if you cannot socialise with your friends and share a cigarette with them?'

Alongside these minor flaws, Frank was an extremely kind and generous man. During my time in Altinure, in the sixties and early seventies, if I needed a car for whatever reason, I had only to ask – a day, a week, a month, take it with you. His faith in my driving skills was not entirely justified. I usually got it back to him in one piece, but I recall one occasion when I got him really worried. I was looking very pale and upset when I returned the car, and I think he assumed I had written it off. In fact, I had just been anointing a little old lady who had burned to death in a house fire, and the rather grim experience had left me a bit pale and shaken.

For a man like Frank to be deprived by sickness of his freedom to come and go would have been an undoubted disaster. He would have found immobility a far greater burden than any sickness, so though we may still wonder why the Lord took him while he was still relatively active and healthy, we can arrive at some understanding of why He took him off so quickly. His death was an enormous shock for Bridie and the boys, but I suspect that, given a choice, this would have been Frank's way to go. He worked hard all his life and suffered severely with the death of Annie and particularly with the death of Ann, but he cared for his family and he served his community in exemplary fashion. He was a good neighbour to everyone. I can only say that I personally will miss him enormously. His death is a loss not merely to Bridie and to his family, but also to this community. It is a loss to this parish of a solid parishioner, a loss that we can ill afford.

We pray that the Lord will speedily forgive any faults in his life, give due recognition to all his goodness, and comfort with his grace all those left behind to mourn him.

Go forth, Christian soul, from this world, in the name of the Almighty Father, who created you, in the name of Jesus, Son of the living God who suffered for you, in the name of the Holy Spirit who was poured out upon you. Go forth faithful Christian. May you see your Redeemer face to face, and enjoy the vision of God for ever. Amen.

Jimmy O'Hara

As we go through life and try to live out our faith we are bound to look around us occasionally and ask what is all this in aid of? Does it make a difference to my life? Am I going to reap some reward that the selfish and irreligious man will not? Or will we both end up unrewarded and unpunished in the soil of the earth for all eternity? All these questions can arise in the course of our lives, and only in the face of death do we begin to see the real significance of the answers.

We all long for eternal life. We want to live forever and we want to share that eternity with those we have loved here on earth, and we quickly realise that we do not have the power to make our own way into heaven. We have to find a saviour, someone who has the power and who will lead the way into heaven and who will show us how our sins can be forgiven and our longing for eternal life can be fulfilled. It is here that the good man, the believing man, comes into his own and reaps the reward of his long years of faithful service to his God and loving care of his family and friends.

Such a man was Jimmy O'Hara. A modest man, a man of faith, a man of talent and generosity, a man of worth and ability, who will be sorely missed, not only by his wife and family but by this parish and the entire community of Limavady and Ballykelly and much, much further afield.

It is exactly fifty years since I first met Jimmy O'Hara. I was appointed curate to ninety-year-old Fr Felix O'Neill in Faughanvale in 1963, and one of my many non-religious duties was to run dances in the newly built St Anne's hall every Friday and Sunday night, a duty that meant not merely booking the band and counting the proceeds but standing in the doorway for the duration to prevent the more ardent supporters of the alcohol business from getting in and preventing the more enthusiastic supporters of other excesses from getting out. And providing a focus for all this high-powered entertainment was the Finvola Seven, the nearest we ever got to a regular house band and composed to a major degree of members of the O'Hara family. I do not recall if Jimmy was the eldest but he was the financial officer and chief negotiator for the band. It was hard-earned money because not merely did the parish always expect a reduction in their fees but the working hours of the musicians defied all good sense and proportion. Instead of coming at a reasonable hour and going home at an equally reasonable hour the patrons wandered in somewhere between ten and eleven o clock and didn't go home until nearly three in the morning. How anyone did a day's work after such a marathon session defies understanding, not to mention the problems associated with keeping Robinsons sand lorry on the road when the driver could barely keep his eyes open. But, as Jimmy has frequently reminded me, we were young and healthy and nothing fazed us. Sleep was for old people, and in the meantime we had a lot of business to get through. We were both twenty-seven at the time, and down the years our common age was a constant source of conversation, especially when it came to dying. The question often arose, who would go first, but I thought to myself last Friday, only Jimmy with his highly developed sense of timing, would have made sure that we parted at the same age by dying on my birthday.

Throughout all of our years of friendship, I doubt that we spent more than ten minutes discussing anything other than music. With my humblest apologies to his wife and family I must admit that they and the rest of the human race took second place, for we rarely discussed anything but music, for Jimmy was a musician of skill and sensitivity who outshone all his rivals. I am taking full account of his modest appraisal of his own abilities but he was in my estimation the best player and interpreter of a slow Irish melody that I have ever heard.

Irish music is not learned. It is absorbed, and as it pours from the heart of the performer it never comes out in a straight line. It curves and bends and drifts past you in a way that defies all musical notation and timing. The world-famous violinist Yehudi Menuhin once tried to play a slow Irish air on an Irish Television programme. It was a disastrous failure, like a man trying to recite poetry in a language he did not understand. Jimmy spoke the language of Irish music instinctively, and those who had even a smattering of the language appreciated his grace and his skill and inevitably ended up telling him that when they died they wanted him to play at their funeral – to which Jimmy had the perfect answer, 'Do you have a date in mind for that engagement?'

One real regret I have is that I do not have any recording of Jimmy's playing, except for a few occasions when he performed with other musicians in Christ the King Church. I often spoke to him about making a CD but in typically modest fashion, he didn't think his performance merited that kind of attention. He was judging it on technical ability and didn't realise that when it came to interpretation he outshone all his rivals. He made numerous television appearances with the band, both north and south of the border, but sadly, none of them seem to have been preserved.

Most of us will know him from his playing at funerals. His performance was always tasteful and melodic, but much as we will miss him as a musician, it is as a gentle friend, a loving husband and father, a loyal parishioner, and a committed believer that he will be missed.

To his wife and his family I offer my deepest sympathy – it is such a short time since he was joyfully celebrating Helen's wedding – we pray that God will strengthen them and console them in the days ahead.

And for Jimmy we pray, that God will recognise all his talents and virtues, that he will speedily forgive any faults, and that he will welcome him into the heavenly choir where he will continue to make music to the greater glory of God for all eternity.

May he rest in peace.

Paul Bateson

We all die before our time, for our time is never quite the same as God's time. We acknowledge that our lives are in God's hands but it is merely an acceptance of the fact that we have limited control over our lives even in the good days, but when the bad days come we have no control whatever. We have heard the warnings of Christ so frequently that they have become part of our culture rather than a part of our faith. And while we are willing to accept that sudden death may affect others, we inject an element of delay into the proceedings when we think about ourselves. We figure the odds against being hit or run over by a bus as we leave church today are pretty slim, so we take a chance and disregard death as long as we can. We find it so hard to accept that we may not live out our lives to a ripe old age; and that is because there is an instinct within everyone that urges us to live forever. The early death, the unforeseen death of someone close to us shatters our plans for eternal life. So we must look around for someone to help us, someone who will keep death at bay for another while and reinforce – if only to the smallest degree – that instinct which cries out for endless life. This miracle man we call our doctor, a suitable title because it means 'a learned man', 'a wise man'. And only a wise and learned man can keep death at bay.

Some would have us think that there is an inevitable conflict between faith and medicine, that one belongs to the realm of the soul and the other to the realm of the body. Not so. In the Catholic Bible there is a book called Ecclesiasticus; in chapter thirty-eight this is what he says about doctors:

Value the services of a doctor for he has his place assigned him by the Lord. His skill comes from the Most High, and he is rewarded by kings. The doctor's knowledge gives him high standing and wins him the admiration of the great. The Lord has created remedies from the earth, and a sensible man will not disparage them. Was not water sweetened by a log, and so the power of the Lord was revealed? The Lord has imparted knowledge to mortals, that by their use of his marvels he may win praise; By means of them the doctor relieves pain. And from them the pharmacist compounds his mixture. There is no limit to the works of the Lord, who spreads health over the whole world. My son, in time of illness do not be remiss, but pray to the Lord and he will heal you.

The miracles of Christ's time are now replicated by modern medicine. Paul Bateson was one of those miracle workers. He enabled the lame to walk and the infirm to stand. He cast out the devils of coronaries and cancer but these are not his real achievements. Many others have worked similar wonders and caused us all to breathe a sigh of relief as we begin to get back on our feet again or to eat and drink once again without any discomfort, but Paul Bateson had a manner and a technique and a dedication to his work that outclassed both colleagues and competitors. The first-time patient was always reassured by the warm and gentle manner. One lady summed it up very succinctly: 'He didn't speak to the ailment. He spoke to the patient.' He instinctively knew from the start what others are only now beginning to realise, that a tense and anxious patient is greatly closed off to healing. That same lady told me that she had gone to him with a lump on her breast, and on her second visit he greeted her with a smile and said, 'I imagine you have found four more since last time', which is exactly what she was convinced she had done. He was not a demonstrative man either with staff or patients. He maintained a calm and methodical approach at all times – even in the midst of crisis – and there were many crises during his working life, the traumas were set aside, the chaos and the disruption in the world around him was not allowed to interfere with work. And the workload that he imposed upon himself was completely unreasonable. It was not measured in hours or days. It was determined by the needs of the patient, and even at the height of the bombing and the wounding and the devastation that we lived through, the work went on and lives were saved. Indeed the major disasters of our time sometimes created a bond of care between consultant and patient that endured right up until the time of his death.

There is so much more that one could say. His patients are a testimony to his skill as a surgeon but it was his personality and his care and his dedication that touched those around him. As one of his co-workers said, 'When Mr Bateson arrived, you knew things were under control.' Outsiders like myself can only admire and indeed envy the care that many individuals received from him on a daily basis. As a father and a husband he will be missed to an enormous degree. The good memories will persevere but they will not take away the pain of loss nor will they fill the empty space that has been created by his death. We pray that the Lord will comfort and strengthen those left behind to mourn him. We pray that he will be accepted into God's kingdom. Whatever faults he may have manifested in his life we pray that they will be speedily forgiven, and that God will grant him that eternal life which we all seek; and that in due course all those who loved him here on earth will be reunited with him again in eternity.

Go forth Christian soul from this world in the name of the Almighty Father who created you, in the name of Jesus Son of the living God who suffered for you, in the name of the Holy Spirit who was poured out upon you, go forth faithful Christian. May you see your redeemer face to face and enjoy the vision of God forever and ever. Amen.

Tommy McDonnell

Someone once said, 'We have no understanding of death until someone close to us dies.' It seems a reasonable statement.

Until Jesus Christ, Our Saviour came on earth death was a mystery. Did everything end with death or was there a new world beyond the grave? Was it a dark and menacing world, or was it a joyful world? Was it eternal and if so how did this come to be? And more and more questions piled up in our minds until Jesus pointed us in the right direction. 'Come to me all you who labour and are overburdened and I will give you rest. Shoulder my yoke and learn from me for I am gentle and humble of heart, and you will find rest for your souls.

For someone like Tommy McDonnell, who was a committed follower of Christ, this joyful vision would have been his basic understanding of death. Throughout his long illness – and that goes back a long way before his hospitalisation – there was no complaint to God and no fear of death. One might say he prayed his way through every crisis. It did not necessarily mean a complete understanding of God's will, but it certainly meant complete faith in God.

In the later years of his life when I knew him, his dedication to his faith was not that of the ordinary parishioner, nor even of the outstanding parishioner. There was a level of commitment that was almost monastic, with attendance at several Masses each day a normal practice, and long hours of private prayer a pattern of his daily life. How much his early life and upbringing contributed to this I cannot say. Certainly his home life would have encouraged dedication to the faith and the Longtower Church would have become a natural base for his spiritual life from his earliest days. But the man himself had a personal chromosome that insisted that everything should be done well, that there was no room for half measures, and that you did not depend on the man – or woman – down the street to set your standards of behaviour or to limit the goal of your achievements.

As a consequence, his activities took him into areas of life that were notable for their disparity, but which never seemed in any way unusual to Tommy and never put the least curb on his hopes and aspirations. He started work as a telegraph boy, delivering messages to the American Base, and getting a glimpse – in the midst of wartime austerity – of the high quality and the plentiful helpings of their cuisine. He was in turn an Air-Raid Warden, a salesman, and finally an Education Welfare Office, but the most intriguing and unexpected activities were not concerned with work. These were his involvement in Amateur Dramatics and Local Politics.

He was chairman of Derry City Nationalist Party, a position that could be classed as the most influential voice in determining the direction of Catholic voting at that time. He was a member of Londonderry Corporation, and along with two other members he took part in the first Ecumenical Service in St Columb's Cathedral in 1967. He was also chairman of People Together, one of the first, if not the first, Ecumenical Group in the city, and he was cashier of the Derry Feis for fifty years.

His involvement in Amateur Dramatics, however, was probably the smartest move he made, because it led indirectly to his meeting and marrying his wife Thelma. He had no real interest in material goods. His family and his principles came first. And all his other interests merely seemed to be a lead-in to his commitment to prayer and devotion in his later life.

He had an abrasive sense of humour, which he frequently tested on his many acquaintances, among them Fr Walter Carolan, who by a strange coincidence died yesterday. They had frequent sparring sessions during their days in Longtower Parish, which extended into their old age in Banagher Parish. One of their more hair-raising encounters involved Fr Carolan tailgating Tommy on the approach road to Feeny at speeds way in excess of the national speed limit. What explanation these two octogenarian adolescents could have offered the authorities for rallying at such speeds on the public highway, I do not know. What I do know is that my sympathies lie with St Peter who now has the dubious privilege of keeping order between the two of them, for nothing is surer than that Fr Carolan will make some derogatory remark when he arrives at the gates of heaven and finds Tommy standing in the gateway, once again collecting the admission fee.

May the bright company of angels bear your soul to paradise.
May the glorious band of Apostles greet you at the gate.
May the white robed army of martyrs welcome you as you come.
May the cheerful throng of saints lighten your heart for ever.
May those you have loved and lost be glad of your coming.
May Mary enfold you in her arms and lead you to Jesus your love forever, and for whom you have longed all this while.
May your home be in the heavenly Jerusalem this day and forever.
Rest in peace, Tommy. God keep you in His care. Amen.

Sean O'Connell

The Book of Wisdom tells us, 'The virtuous man, though he die before his time, will find rest,' a promise that is easily accepted. He has left behind the pains and disappointments of life, the straining hopes that are not fulfilled, the anxious verdicts that bring fears about the future and the struggle to keep a brave front in the face of adversity. That is all now finished and he rests in peace. He awaits the full vision of God in the joy of eternal life. The virtuous man indeed will find rest.

For those left behind to mourn him it is a different and a sadder story. For them rest is still a long way off; there is for the present only the struggle to come to terms with God's will; to accept that someone who has been an intimate part of their lives has been called away.

For myself, my first memory of Sean O'Connell dates back, I think, to 1949 when we were both serving time in a military-type educational establishment called St Columb's College. Unlike Lord Archer we got no parole and no time off for good behaviour, and any excursions outside the boundary fence were regarded as escape attempts and punished accordingly, so football within the perimeters of our living-space figured fairly high in our list of recreations. In fact, if memory serves me it was our only real recreation, but I cannot recall that Sean's skills in this field had begun to reveal themselves to any great extent at this stage. However, the deft footwork and lightning reflexes must have been gearing up because I do remember his big brother telling me that while at home on holiday they were washing the dishes – or rather big brother was washing and Sean was drying – and as a wet plate was passed from washer to dryer it slipped towards the floor, but before it could hit the ground Sean had got his toe under it and flicked it into the air and caught it on the way down. The only possible weakness in this story is that big brother has never been known to wash dishes either before or since that occasion.

Sean's footballing skills, however, soon manifested themselves and before long he was known the length and breadth of the country simply as Sean O'Connell the footballer, regardless of what other interest or vocation he might have been following at the time. But he was more than just a footballer. He was an elegant footballer. Some people can get results by hustling and pushing and scrabbling for the ball. Sean was never less than stylish and graceful. But style and grace were always a part of him. No later than yesterday a middle aged lady told me that in his heyday she and her friends followed him around the country to football matches for, as she so succinctly put it, 'We thought he was just gorgeous.' And for myself, I could only wonder that someone who was only one year younger than me could look twenty-one years younger. I eventually concluded that 1936 must have been a particularly tough year, but a sympathetic clerical colleague explained it to me by saying that if Sean had been twenty-one years older than me he would have still looked younger and better.

It was, therefore, not entirely surprising that when I came to Limavady I should find him here thirty years on completely unchanged – the original picture of Dorian Gray – with a wife and a grown up family, but what I found hard to accept was that in addition to all the other joys of his situation in life he was now retired for several years while I was just about to take up a new job instead of enjoying a well-earned rest.

And that was how the picture remained, one of idyllic happiness and relaxed retirement until three years ago when alarm bells began to ring. Happily, things were not quite as menacing as first appeared and for the next two years he coped quietly and gently as always, but anxiety was never far from the door, and in more recent times the sickness returned with worrying severity. Margaret tried every possible intervention, physical, spiritual and emotional and every source of healing and intercession was invoked and every crisis was met with a positive and determined attitude, 'We keep on trying to the very end.' If God's mind could have been changed it would have been changed for he was besieged on all sides with relentless prayer and intercession, but it was not to be. Sean had lived his life and now the Lord was calling him home. And as he had lived so he died quietly and courageously, conceding the victory to God.

We give thanks to God for his life; we applaud its many achievements and seek forgiveness for any failures. We know that it has brightened this world for the short time it has been here and now we return it to the Almighty who created it.

Go forth Christian soul out of this world in the name of God the Almighty Father who created you, in the name of Jesus Christ Son of the Living God who suffered for you, in the name of the Holy Spirit who was poured out upon you, go forth faithful Christian. Amen.

Sammy Mulgrew

The words of the first readings strike a chord with most people and yet the meaning is not altogether clear. The writer is called Quoheleth, son of David, and in general he is not a very happy man, so we wonder when he says that 'there is a time for war and a time for peace and a time to live and a time to die', is he saying that there is a good time to die and a good time to go to war, or is he just saying that death happens and wars happen and our lives have to accommodate them?

Certainly it would seem to us at first that there is not a good time to die, that death is an evil and there is no favourable time to greet him. But then we think a little deeper and call to mind even our limited experience of death and we realise that some deaths are much more acceptable than others. It is the approach of death that inevitably frightens us. We wonder how it will come about. Will it be painful? Will we feel very lonely? How will we know that we are going to die? To be spared all these anxieties must surely make for an easier death, and that is how it is with those who slip quietly from life to death without warning. A parishioner who died recently said a short time before she died that she no longer feared death because she had collapsed of a heart attack some time previously and it was like going to sleep. She said she had no awareness of how or when she had lost consciousness. It was a completely painless experience.

For Sammy Mulgrew death must have been equally quiet and painless, and had he known that we were grounding our thoughts on the Book of Ecclesiastes he would have taken grave exception for no two men were ever quite so different as Quoheleth, the son of David and Sammy Mulgrew. Quoheleth was a pessimist, almost a depressive. Everything was a vanity, a waste of time; there was nothing new or exciting under the sun. Everything had been tried before and found wanting. Sammy, on the other hand, not merely enjoyed life; he brought joy into other people's lives. The world and its people fascinated him and simple things caught his attention and entertained him. He never travelled very far afield, but he enjoyed the life that he led and the people that he knew. He was a solid worker all his days beginning with feeding a stone breaker at fourteen years of age and then progressing through various jobs until his career with the Water Service. He was an enthusiastic singer – from his days with the Finvola Showband until his final performance with the choir on Sunday morning for the opening of St Mary's, and all the countless performances in between. He was also a dedicated football supporter, not just of Manchester United, but of the local clubs which he supported by doing all kinds of jobs for them. But it was as a man of humour that he really shone.

He had a beautifully refined sense of the ridiculous that could pick up a good story in the same way that his ear could pick up a good song. He would sidle up behind you, put his arm round your shoulder and ask did you ever hear the one about this or that. But it was never a straight-forward joke. It always had the sting in the tail that you were never expecting. His humour was more of a shaggy-dog-story type than a straight-forward-joke type. In fact, you really need to hear his stories to appreciate his humour, so if you'll excuse me, I'm going to do what I have never done before. I am going to tell a funny story at a funeral, but only because it is one of Sammy's funny stories. And I might say before I begin that he didn't worry too much about political correctness.

An Englishman was taking six monkeys to the zoo and his lorry breaks down. Paddy is driving past in his transit van and he stops to see what is wrong. The Englishman asks him, 'Would you take these monkeys to the zoo and I'll give you a hundred pounds?' And Paddy readily agrees. He sets them into the front seat of the transit, so they can have a good view of the road and off he goes.

Several hours later the Englishman has his lorry fixed and he heads up the road in the direction of the zoo and who does he meet but Paddy coming in the opposite direction with the six monkeys still lined along the front seat of the transit van. He flags Paddy down and says to him, 'I thought you said you would take them to the zoo.' Paddy replies, 'I took them to the zoo, but I had twenty pound left over so now I am taking them to the pictures.'

A man with that kind of humour will be sorely missed. Not just by his sisters and brothers but by the choir members and football teams and supporters and indeed by everyone who knew him because he brought sunshine into all of our lives. I have no doubt whatever that Sammy will go straight to heaven. Death did not catch him by surprise. He prepared for it every day and that is why he died with his rosary beads in his hand. There may be a certain delay at the gates of heaven because I think inevitably when Sammy meets St Peter he will put his arm around his shoulder and say to him, 'Did you ever hear the story about the man from Ardgarvan?' And the business of heaven will be put on hold until Sammy tells one more of his stories. After that he will seek out the heavenly choir and he will join them in giving praise and worship to God for the rest of eternity.

May his kindly soul rest in peace. May any faults that he has committed be speedily forgiven and may all the joy that he brought to people here on earth be recognised by God and may he know happiness for ever in the kingdom of heaven. Amen.

Annie Conway

Among the many blessings that we ask from God is the blessing of a long and happy life, even though it is not what we really want. It is not that we would ever think of rejecting such a gift, indeed, we will be most grateful for it, but it does not measure up to our needs and expectations; for the longest and happiest life will always come to an end some day, and that limitation frightens us, for we do not know what lies ahead. Indeed, we do not know if anything lies ahead, or rather, we did not know until Christ came and not merely showed us the way into a new life, but led the way himself, so that where he had gone we would hope to follow. Nothing less than eternal life will satisfy us. Nothing but the knowledge that the life we live is going to continue eternally will give us happiness. Of course we get caught up in the affairs of the world and the necessities of life on this earth, and we seem to grow busier every day, so that our good intentions of looking beyond this world and heeding the words of Christ and trying to prepare ourselves for this much more important life gets put on the long finger, and only the decline of our bodies and the growing awareness of death compels us to turn to God and try to make up for lost time. That is how most of us deal with life and death.

But there are a few who listen to the teaching of Christ, and who try to put it into action, not just at the last moment, but all through their lives, and they are the real examples. They are the real saints.

Such a one was Annie Conway. She would probably be horrified to hear herself described in such terms, but it was that humility, that dedication to her duties and responsibilities as a Christian wife, mother and neighbour, that made her stand out even among other well-intentioned Christians. Let me give you an example. When I heard of her death I mentioned it to a friend of mine, but I was unsure if she knew who I was talking about. She said she not merely knew who I was talking about, but that she remembered her vividly from the one and only time she met her almost forty years ago. Her hospitality, her caring approach to strangers, her anxiety to make sure that they were at their ease and did not feel in any way left out, impressed her so much that she remembered her immediately and had no problem knowing who I was talking about, but the really strange thing was that Annie's death saddened her in a way that the death of far more familiar friends had not done.

On a personal level, I cannot even begin to recount the care and the kindness and the patience and the tolerance that she showed to me and all the other clergy that came about this parish. It was not just the occasional visit or cup of tea. It was like having a permanent boarder in the house – and a non-paying boarder, at that. When we were not being fed in her kitchen we were being stocked up by her husband, Patsy, with all the produce of his garden. And when Patsy wasn't available, so Michael tells me, we went into the garden and stole it. We were so used to being pampered in those days that it never occurred to us that cooking and caring for a husband and five children was a big enough assignment without having to slot the local curate into the equation. All of which was outrageously demanding, but we even imposed other people on her, on the principle, I suppose, that if you want something done you go to the busiest person in the parish. Certainly, we added to her labours without ever thinking of the awesome burdens we were laying upon her shoulders. I recall one of the Sisters of Nazareth telling me that she had organised holidays for all the children in her care, but for one reason or another, one of the host families had to cancel, so that one child was going to be left behind while the rest went on holidays. Could I help in any way? I probably didn't ask myself if there was anyone with more time on their hands and less responsibilities. I simply landed down to Annie, put the situation to her, and another responsibility was added to Annie's many already existing responsibilities.

She had wonderful health all her days, and in view of the loving care she bestowed upon everybody, she certainly needed it. Her attention was never focused on herself. It was always a question of how she could be of service to other people. It was in fact the realisation on a heroic level of the commandment to love one's neighbour. As for loving God, she had the same humble, unpretentious, but absolutely genuine relationship with God as she had with her neighbour. Her spiritual life is summed up beautifully in a sentiment expressed by her daughter Elizabeth. 'The condition of Annie's rosary beads', she says, 'reflected her attitude to life: "It'll do grand." The plain wooden beads were held together by a safety pin. However, they were very precious to her. The rosary beads were the first thing she looked for in the morning, and the last thing she touched at night.'

She was greatly blessed to be able to spend her last years at home, for her health had begun to decline and she was no longer able to care for herself, but her children rallied around her and saw to it that all her needs were attended to at home. Though it was never easy to determine her needs for her steady chorus when someone tried to attend her was 'I'm grand. I'm all right'. Her family will miss her, not because of what she could do – for that was limited in recent years – but because of her powerful presence. She affected the lives of all who came in contact with her, none more so than her family, so her absence will affect them more than anyone else. The focus around which their lives revolved for so long has now departed, and they will find the vacuum very hard to fill. Time will ease the pain somewhat, but nothing will replace the sense of loving security which her presence generated throughout their lives.

This family has lost a loving mother. This parish has lost a wonderful parishioner. And all of us have lost the warmth and the example of a truly Christian neighbour.

Eternal rest grant unto her Lord and let perpetual light shine upon her. May her soul and the souls of all the faithful departed through the mercy of God rest in peace. Amen.

John McAtamney

'In my Father's house are many rooms. I am going now to
prepare a place for you and after I have gone and prepared
you a place I shall return to take you with me ...'

The word 'serendipity' is not a common part of our daily speech –
for obvious reasons – but there are occasions when it comes in
useful. It basically means the knack or the gift of making good
decisions, good choices, without having to think them through;
one might say the ability to make the right decisions by accident.
If you have this ability you have the gift of serendipity. The
example I usually employ to explain it is the lady who went
camping in Donegal and had to find a doctor for a sick child in the
middle of the night in a completely unfamiliar landscape. She
followed the lights and knocked on the door of the first house she
came to and asked where she could find a doctor. The householder
answered, 'You can have your pick. There are seven of them inside
playing poker.'

In the same way, I think, serendipity has come into play this
morning because the gospel, which is part of today's feast of All
Souls, celebrates variety; it celebrates differentiation; and no gospel
could be more appropriate or more suitable for the funeral of John
McAtamney, for John was a man who resisted all efforts to make
him conform to the ways of those around him, or to make him the
same as anyone else. God, in his wisdom, has made us all different
– even in physical appearance. Where human beings rejoice in their
efforts to clone someone else, to produce a perfect copy of another
human being, God rejoices in His ability to make us all different.

He finds no joy in repeating himself. He would find it boring and unproductive. And He made us all different, not so that we would all clash with one another, but so that we might learn from our differences. I can learn nothing from a man who is an exact copy of myself. I can only learn from someone who is different from me. But, as human beings, we admire conformity. We urge one another to accept the same rules of behaviour, to dress the same as one another, to eat the same kind of food, to build the same kind of houses and to watch the same entertainment, because it is neater and tidier and more easy to control than the world of the maverick and the rebel.

Many of you will have known John when he was a young man, or even when he was in his childhood. Most of us, however, have only known him in recent years, and we all know from hard experience that we do not improve with age. We become more belligerent, more assertive, more impatient, more pressing in our demands to have things done our way, and less sensitive to the needs of those who care for us. And so, some of us may not have encountered John in the prime of his days. The academic and athletic abilities of his youth were things of the past, but the imprint was still there, and we tend to forget that our talents and our abilities are often much harder to carry than our limitations. John was not good at physical or mental inactivity. He needed to be going somewhere. He needed to be doing something. And eventually he reached the point where he did his own thing and travelled his own journeys regardless of the opinions of those around him. These were not ideal guidelines for holding down any job, and they certainly did nothing to enhance his performance as a sacristan.

Even so, minor failings in this direction might have been overlooked had he not insisted on demanding the attention of the local clergy at what was by any standards unsociable hours. Fr Downey used to say that it was not so much being wakened at 2.30 a.m. by John looking for a cigarette, as the fact that he had told John, most emphatically, on several occasions previously, that he did not smoke, that he had never smoked and had no intention of starting smoking and consequently did not have, and would not have in the future, any cigarettes.

On a domestic level he could be quite single-minded, but no one was ever really able to follow his reasoning. We all knew, however, that if matters on the domestic front were not meeting his expectations, he became quite agitated and took a sudden and inexplicable vengeance on the furniture and the internal doors.

This is not to say that he was an unlikeable person. As any husband will testify, there are people who can drive you demented but for some reason you still continue to love them. Well, a lot of people seemed to love John. I'm not saying they necessarily liked him all the time, but they loved him in that they forgave him, and rescued him, and cared for him, and even despaired of him.

Of all who cared for him no one was more loving than his sister Gene. In fact, I did not hesitate to warn her that she would ruin her own health if she continued attending him with such dedication, but it never really made any difference. Gene continued to give, and John continued to take, for that was the nature of both of them.

To come back to the gospel that we started with: Jesus assures us that there are many rooms in his Father's house, rooms for all the different personalities that He has created, for eternity would be a mighty dull place if we were all to be the same. John retained his individuality more effectively than the rest of us, and that, we can only admire, but it was a two-edged sword. He did not listen to the wisdom of others, and so he continued to walk the roads amid heavy traffic in the hours of darkness both North and South of the border, and no one could persuade him to do otherwise. His tragic death has been painful for everyone, for his family and friends who cared for him for so many years, for the driver of the car, for those who tried to convince him of the dangers on the roads, and for those who knew him for so many years as a unique member of their community.

We pray that the Lord will accept him into his kingdom, with all his varied traits of personality and behaviour, and there grant him eternal rest. Amen.